Frederic Dan Huntington

Forty days with the Master

Frederic Dan Huntington

Forty days with the Master

ISBN/EAN: 9783337268916

Printed in Europe, USA, Canada, Australia, Japan

Cover: Foto ©Andreas Hilbeck / pixelio.de

More available books at **www.hansebooks.com**

FORTY DAYS WITH THE MASTER.

FORTY DAYS
WITH THE MASTER

BY

BISHOP HUNTINGTON

OF CENTRAL NEW YORK.

NEW YORK
E. P. DUTTON & COMPANY
31 West 23d Street
1891

In form and general plan this volume may be regarded as completing a series of three, including "Helps to a Holy Lent" and "New Helps to a Holy Lent." In those two, many of the subjects obviously pertaining to the meditations, self-examinations and active duties of this yearly appointment are presented in their particulars. What follows is published with a desire on the part of the writer to extend the help, if possible, and to share with others convictions that have grown in his own mind as to certain truths lying at the heart of the Faith and Church of Christ, as to the relations of men and society to His Person and Kingdom, and as to divine powers which are at work in the world, too little observed, but of deep import both to personal religious health and to social righteousness. According to any comprehensive idea of Lent it would seem that its states of feeling and its rules and practice of discipline can have no proper end or meaning apart from their use as serious aids to the building of character.

F. D. H.

Syracuse,
Advent, 1890,

FORTY DAYS WITH THE MASTER.

Ash-Wednesday.

FIRST LAW AND FIRST FAILURE.

LENT comes to lead us into liberty, that only real liberty with which Christ makes free. In the long dispute between those who hold that the power of religion is faith in the Sovereignty of God and those who would find it in the work of man, the two schools have really at heart a common ground of their beliefs. Both systems hold that man is not to live for himself, if he would live forever. Both are torn from their root, in the truth and in the cross, if they forget this inmost law of the kingdom, which is the liberty of Christ. In the acceptance of this radical principle of self-renunciation the great divergent parties of Grace and Service may be reconciled. Whether I count it my first duty and first joy to do the will of God, or to adore Him because

He does His will in the blessedness of men, my way is the same; it is to live in a chosen, disinterested and glad obedience to Him who is God and Man. Christianity is self-sacrifice. These Forty Days with the Master have their warrant in helping us to be the Master's servants, though He is so gracious as to call us not so much His servants as His friends. This builds character, and character, so far as you are concerned personally, is the end of all the provisions and services of the Church. Church buildings, ministers, parishes and missions, public worship, sacraments, sermons, singing, Lent, a prayer-book, a Bible, are the strong array of Christian helps and instruments. No one of them, or the sum of them all taken together, is an end to itself. We cannot understand this too well, or remember it too often. Provided in their highest perfection they would be a failure if they did not make some man, or men, or women righteous. It is an insidious tendency of all visible institutions to put themselves in place of the original power that created them, to hide out of sight the life from which they spring, and to mistake the apparatus for something better still, something nobler, more precious, and more essential, beneath it. The Church regarded as most men see it, humanly, is one of these visible institutions, having this human danger along with its divine glory. Christ, who created it, and brought it into the world as the working organ of His own divine life, spent a great deal of time and teaching in pointing out the fatal mischiefs of this mistake. Over and over again He warns us against substituting what is superficial and perishable, even in religion, for what is solid and eternal; professions for conduct; the "I go, sir," for the going; the tools and ornaments of the Temple for Him who alone makes the Temple holy; the priest's official dignity for his steady, self-sacrificing service. What He wants us to see is that, while both the parts are sacred, one without the other is a delusion, and may be a lie. People blunderingly disparage the Church when what they have in mind is that one of the Church's two sons who misrepresents her by giving her the signs and starts of life without constant obedience. We all know the difference between spirit and body when we *see* a body after the life has left it. But you do not honor your faulty friend by putting contempt on his body, or save even a fruitless tree by cutting away its trunk. "Make the tree good." Christian character is to be formed and ripened according to the plan of God, not in ways of our devising, but under His own laws, in His own kingdom, which is His Church.

But the power of the Church is the personal power of its Head. Affectionate and trusty loyalty to a leader is a very different thing from adherence to a set of speculative opinions; it is a far more inspiring thing. Again and again attempts have been made, on the basis of rational philosophy, to construct a scheme of moral obligation or righteous conduct independently of Jesus of Nazareth, this Son of God and Son of Man. That has been the undertaking of nearly a dozen "Religions." Their effect on the living forces of mankind, the heart, the will, the conscience of the actual world, as compared with the personal power of a divine yet human Saviour, is that of moonlight compared with sunlight, or as a set of rules and a volume of poetry compared with the benignant and vital authority of a living Lord, not the less manly for His divinity, in whom love and wisdom are blended. Christianity is alone in this embodiment of all its living and loving force in Him whom Christians worship, love and serve. If your religious course begins with a personal devotion and conversion to Him it will be faithful as He is faithful, constant and abiding as He is constant and abiding, steadfast with His steadfastness who is the same yesterday, to-day, and forever. It will be a satisfying service, because affectionate and hearty.

Spiritual physicians, who have had the care of souls, will agree that most of the unhappy people that come to them, lamenting their lack of religious life, give this account of themselves: There was a time when they were aroused; they heard a voice asking why they were sent into the world and saying, "Go work in God's vineyard;" they saw a vision of heavenly light. But this interest was fitful, not constant; the better hour fled and left no mark; the vision vanished, and self and the world came back. Repentance was the early dew; resolve was the morning cloud. It is remarkable that the first book written, a picture of a thinking man's experience under the hand of God, has in it the same confession that serious minds of every age since have repeated: "O that I were as in months past, when God's candle shined upon my head, and by His light I walked through darkness, and the secret of God was upon my tabernacle!" Remember our spiritual life is under laws, like our bodies, the seasons, and the growing grain. Unless we mind them and work as they work, church-going, preaching, and Lent-keeping are in vain. You are supposed not to be trifling now, but in earnest.

Ask then with what idea as to its purpose, and what motive as to its personal effect, your religious interest began. One principal cause of failure is found in false expectations. Whether we look into the Master's teaching in the New Testament, or into the practical embodiment of it in His life, we find the chief mark upon it to be that it is unselfish. His aim is to carry us, in our chief concerns, out of ourselves. Just so far as thought, labor, feeling, anxiety are fixed on our own comfort, narrowed down to the little circle of our private welfare, even in the matter of religion, we have mistaken the essential quality and first law of His Gospel. Men may be self-seeking, self-pleasing and self-complacent in religion as well as in trade, or society, or study, or amusement. In the false religious systems of the world that spirit has been uppermost; worship and obedience were rendered for a selfish advantage, to selfish deities living in a selfish heaven. However splendid the ritual, or costly the sacrifice, the devotion was a calculation, and the sacrifice a bribe. Christ said prayer and praise are a child's free-will offering of beautiful faith to a Father; the first and last act of a

Church in these American States is puny, slow, small, failing of its possible conquests and promised glories, it is because Christian worshippers are not enlarged and quickened by this ennobling and enabling spirit of the kingdom, as Christ brought it, a mission on the earth. It is safe, it is salvation, to live in the kingdom by the law of the King. There is no other salvation, no other life eternal. Personal responsibility for the welfare of the world about you is a chief element in the vitality and stability of your own faith—not the great, far-off world, so distant as to be indistinct, or so general as to be unreal, but the near, actual, living world of men and women. Have you pondered the problems that perplex them, bewilder them and set some of them to asking why they were ever born into the world, and whether suicide would not be a pardonable escape out of it? Has it struck you that in this time, in this country, in this community, where wrong, and cunning, and lying, and unbelief, and the desecration of holy things, and fascinating but poisonous books circulating clandestinely among your children in the schools, are pulling down the only safeguards that can make homes pure, marriages sacred, society decent, and the future tolerable,—it is an awful thing to live at all? If not, then surely it is no wonder that your past religion seems to you little better than the phantasm of an idle brain, and your expectation of heaven an unsubstantial dream. It is only by looking at these neighbors as Christ looked at His, only with a burning sense that it is your mind and your heart, your work and will, your pity and your time, that can save them—them and you together,—only in this way that what you have ventured to call your faith can be an inspiring and satisfying thing.

"Thou knowest, Lord, the weariness and sorrow
Of the sad heart that comes to Thee for rest;
Cares of to-day and burdens of to-morrow,
Blessings implored, and sins to be confessed.
I come before Thee at Thy gracious word,
And lay them at Thy feet; Thou knowest, Lord!
Thou knowest all the past; how long and blindly
On the dark mountains the lost wanderer strayed,
How the Good Shepherd followed, and how kindly
He bore it home, upon His shoulders laid,
And healed the bleeding wounds, and soothed the pain,
And brought back life, and hope, and strength again."

O ALMIGHTY and most merciful Lord God, look down from heaven, we beseech Thee, as we draw near unto Thee with lowly penitence. We entreat Thee to forgive us all our offences, and to receive us as Thy dear children. Let Thy

Fatherly Hand ever be over us, and so loosen our chains, O Lord, and deliver our souls from the snares and temptations of this evil world, that by Thy same merciful and most powerful Hand we may be for ever united to Thee through Thy only-begotten Son, Who is our pardon and our peace. Grant this for Thine own Love's sake, in Him, Christ our Lord. *Amen.*

First Thursday.

THE MASTER'S TWO-FOLD CALL.

KNOWING perfectly that in His ultimate purpose He was to form and perpetuate a Society which should be the organization of His Spirit, the most vital and powerful "Body" ever existing on the earth, it is remarkable how personal our Lord was in all the first acts of His ministry. He not only called, taught, and trained persons, but it seems to have been His intention so to constitute this Society that all the social and political combinations of His time should be crossed and broken up by it, classes fused, their dividing lines obliterated, and the individuality of every individual preserved. See how he took His countrymen as they came,—sailors, farmers, a physician, office-holders, all more interested at first in their pursuits than in Him. What is it that He seeks first to do? To draw each person to Himself, so as to establish a direct personal communication, or an infusing of the divine life into the man; not that sort of conversion which would destroy our personality and substitute another, but a careful preservation of the personal characteristic and variety, and yet the forming within of the image, the spiritual and living image of the Master. Perfect man Himself He reaches into every heart and puts His strong and tender hand on something there that needs Him—on a publican's longing for sympathy, on Peter's impulses, on John's enthusiasm, on Thomas's doubts, on Nathaniel's purity, —on one woman's sorrow, and another's shame, and another's gratitude. This was the secret of His power. He knew just where to touch. The object is to link each heart to His own, to make them all see the Father's face as He sees it, to make them hate sin, and believe in charity, and hunger and thirst after righteousness. They will come to this by keeping Him company. They will not only learn it from Him, but catch it from Him, or breathe it in. All through the early part of His three years' ministry, this is His work,—calling, gathering, attracting and inspiring. He is preparing a few men to do a certain thing.

They have a special name, suited to what is going on, "disciples." After a while the name changes, because the work changes. They are not *called*, but *sent*; not gathered, but scattered; not only learners, but preachers and laborers.

They go to all quarters of the globe. They are apostles now. Illuminated, they become Light-bearers. They have found out that no man liveth to himself, or dieth to himself. Watch them, and you see rising up in them the great conception of a cause or kingdom. They are to live for that. The idea takes possession of them and masters their minds. They see Christ in this "Cause." They have a passion for it, because it is His. Their loyalty to His Person becomes one with their devotion to His Church. It is His Body. Knowing it, they know Him. It is His House. Spreading it, they widen His glory. The sense of personal responsibility enlarges; it passes from concern for their own salvation to concern for the saving of the world. They no longer inquire how many there are with them, but only where each shall go and what each shall do; not what are the prospects of success, but where there is room for work. They are lifted into a higher view, and their standard of duty is raised with them. Their piety becomes unselfish, their life is missionary life. Freely they have received; freely they give themselves away. Every man knows that he must answer for the triumph of the cause. The live coal has touched their lips. The voice of the Lord was heard saying, "Whom shall I send, and who shall go?" Then said each believer and follower of the Crucified, "Here am I; send me."

All along, that divine fire has flamed up in some single heart, wherever the cause has been set forward, or great things have been done. It was because St. Philip felt personally responsible for the souls in Samaria that he went out from Jerusalem, the first missionary, with the whole weight of the honor of the Church on his shoulders. St. Peter traveled with the same power of solitary and personal responsibility. St. Paul felt it and acted under it everywhere, and it made him the greatest of missionaries, the greatest of theologians, the greatest of preachers. St. Luke felt it when he stood by his master at Rome, while others deserted, so that Paul wrote of him in the epistle, "Only Luke is with me." The whole Christian age has passed. How is it now?

Within our own life-time two men have left England and home, each conscious of personal responsibility for the salvation of a continent, saying, "Send me," and going to the ends to the earth. Bishop Selwyn sailed to New Zealand because others counted their lives too dear to go; and the doors of an immortal future for nations sitting in darkness opened before him. Livingstone felt his way by faith to the heart of Africa; and now the Kingdom of Heaven is pressing after him, to seek two hundred millions of people. Not long before he died, alone there, for the eye of God, he wrote in his journal, "My Jesus, my King, my Life, my All! I have given and here dedicate my whole life to Thee. Accept me, and grant that before this year has gone I may finish my task. Amen." When his body was found dead it was on its knees.

These seem like prophets and evangelists, distant figures, too far on and far up for our following. But remember that for every one like them God wants ten thousand Christians faithful in ordinary places; and He wants one in the place where you are. You are not to go to the Southern Ocean, but to bear the witness of a devout, patient, sweet-tempered housemate in the house where you go in and out. You are to conquer for Christ the barren waste in your own heart, your Africa. Remember those commanding spirits were at first unworthy and of small account. They would have been insignificant to the end, and we should never have heard their names, if they had not answered, each one, to the Master's call, "Here am I; send me."

And because it will lift you up a little nearer to them, and will stir you with fresh energy to holier work, hear Isaiah's description of his vision. "In the year that King Uzziah died, I saw the Lord sitting upon a throne high and lifted up, and His train filled the temple. Above it stood the seraphim. Each one had six wings; with twain he covered his face, and with twain he covered his feet, and with twain he did fly. And one cried unto another and said, Holy, holy, holy is the Lord of Hosts; the whole earth is full of His glory. And the bolts of the door moved at the voice of Him that cried, and the house was filled with smoke. Then said I, Woe is me! for I am undone; because I am a man of unclean lips and I dwell in the midst of a people of unclean lips; for mine eyes have seen the King, the Lord of Hosts. Then flew one of the seraphim unto me, having a live coal in his hand, which he had taken with the tongs from off the altar. And he laid it upon my mouth, and said, Lo, this hath touched thy lips, and thine iniquity is taken away, and thy sin purged. Also I heard the voice of the Lord, saying, Whom shall I send, and who will go for us? Then said I, Here am I; send me."

"Few years, no wisdom, no renown,
Only my life can I lay down;
Only my heart, Lord, to Thy throne
I bring! and pray
That child of Thine I may go forth,
And spread glad tidings through the earth,
And teach sad hearts to know Thy worth—
Lord, here am I!

"And make me strong; that staff, and stay,
And guide, and guardian of the way.
To Theeward may I bear each day
Some precious soul.
'Speak, for I hear!' make 'pure in heart'
Thy face to see. Thy truth impart
In hut and hall, in church and mart—
Lord, here am I!

"I ask no heaven till earth be Thine,
Nor glory-crown while work of mine
Remaineth here. When earth shall shine
Among the stars,
Her sins wiped out, her captives free,
Her voice a music unto Thee—
For crown, new work give Thou to me;
Lord, here am I!"

BE present, O Lord, to our supplications, nor let thy merciful clemency be far away from us. Grant, we beseech Thee, that renewing our sacred observances with annual devotion we may please Thee both in body and soul. Give a salutary effect to our fasting, that the mortification of our flesh may prove the nourishment of our souls. May thy mercy, O Lord, be beforehand with thy servants, and all our iniquities be blotted out by thy speedy pardon; through Jesus Christ our Lord. *Amen.*

First Friday.

TWO WASHINGS.

We shall deal effectually with our moral life very much in proportion as we understand its laws. Like the body, the spirit has its laws of growth, health, welfare and restoration from disease. They are less plain and more complicated; they are not reached by the senses; but we come to know the inward man as we know the outward, by observation, by attention, by study. We can shirk spiritual discipline; but we cannot, if we shirk it, be wise, safe or strong.

One of the facts to be found out is that in the renewal of the soul's life there is one that is principal, and there are others that are subordinate. One is supreme, in that the others are not likely to take place to much purpose without it; it is radical, in that it goes to the root (*radix*) of character, altering by our will the quality of all that grows from the root, or the whole of life; it is comprehensive, in that the effect of it is to touch and change for the better the various purposes of the will and the entire course of conduct. Other renewals may follow. They must if this is real. "The inward man is renewed day by day." Religious nurture implies a succession of religious acts; but there is a beginning of them which is apt to be conscious and intentional. Character-building is a process of repeated strokes, shapings, convictions; but before them all is the laying of a foundation. As often as we wander we must mark the deviation and come back to the right way; but the general direction is chosen and taken at the outset.

What is now referred to is not the doctrinal distinction between regeneration and conversion. The sacramental mystery of a second birth by the grace of the Spirit of God acting on an obedient human faith, set fast by our Lord and His Apostles in the original constitution of the Divine Kingdom, is a reality apart from the personal decisions that follow it. What secret connection there may be, or how it may be traced in different individuals, is not here considered. The mystic "wind bloweth where it listeth, and thou canst not tell whence it cometh, or whither it goeth." In adult baptism the connection between the personal choice and the grace conferred is very close. But among those movements of the will which are properly called a conversion there is one, with many and perhaps with most persons, which is readily distinguished by its definiteness, its immediate power, its permanent reforming impression. Not a few of us in retrospect can fix it in time and place. There was a full stop on a wrong road. The face was set in a new direction. There was an extrication from a tangled web of sophistries and confusions. A fog lifted. An obstinate habit was broken short off. It is not too much to say that life became a new thing and put on a new look. Throughout the New Testament this change is constantly recognized and is sanctioned by such names as "turning," "arising," "awaking," being "renewed in the spirit of the mind." Between this and "amendment," or "improvement," or repentances for particular sins, or the correcting of daily errors, there is a difference.

In one of the striking actions of His ministry Christ marks this difference, symbolizing it first in His attitude and gesture, and then interpreting it in language. The most impulsive of His disciples, from mingled shame and pride, refuses the foot-washing:

and then, seeing that consent will be a proof of loyal devotion, breaks out in a characteristic exclamation of superfluous submission, "Lord, not my feet only, but also my hands and my head." With that even dignity which will never suffer a breeze of emotion to sway the balances of truth this way or that, never will be elated by a gush of sentiment, or depressed by the dullest unbelief, Christ at once abashes and instructs him: "He that is washed needeth not save to wash his feet, but is clean every whit." There is a contrast in the words Christ used keener, more concise and more complete than the English represents. Two verbs instead of one make the Greek antithesis vivid and beautiful. He that has been washed as the bather is washed needs not now to have that chief and general cleansing repeated. In the world of spiritual things there is a heavenly order. Everything in its place; one step at a time; duties are not to be jumbled together; effusiveness to-day will not make up for the self-occupied sullenness, or wilfulness, or greediness of yesterday. Learn, Simon Peter, that defect is not cured by excess. Every command must be met as it comes. Every offence must cost you a fresh sacrifice of self-sufficiency. A single ablution from hereditary or past iniquity will not cleanse you from this frequent defilement; nor will it excuse you from humiliation, confession, and prayer for pardon, as often as you let temptation stain your heart. Duties are not measured by their dimensions; the small are sometimes the hardest tests of a true discipleship. You are my disciple already; you forsook the world for me; you chose me when I chose you. But you are not beyond the danger of repeated fallings away from that high consecration. We live in a dirty world. We travel on a dusty highway. We breathe a poisoned air. Society is full of contagions. An enemy lurking within conspires with the enemy that lurks on the right hand and the left. Once you had to be changed from bad to good,—in the main purpose, the ruling motive, the prevailing drift, the deliberate aim; you have yet to be changed from good to better. Even the branch that beareth fruit must be purged—purged painfully—that it may bring forth more fruit.

It follows that it is a special spur to increasing vigilance and every-day faithfulness if a great act of renewal—a self-consecration graciously owned and accepted by the consecrating Spirit—has once broken the force of the tyrant tempter, once turned your face from the dark to the light, once set your feet in a large place, once delivered you from a base bondage into the glorious liberty of a son, or daughter, of God. To have been lifted over from a faithless because careless indifference to a foothold on the side of Christ is indeed to hold a vantage-ground of immense superiority. Worldliness itself cannot deny that, however its frivolity may laugh off the secret conviction, or its cynicism sneer at the weak convert's inconsistencies. Madame Sevigne, from her rank, beauty and brilliancy, was a favorable example of the better sort of Parisian womanhood in the seventeenth century. Her feeling about religion was an uncultivated instinct. Impiety against her Maker was a rather more dreadful danger than an affront to the court or a violation of its fashions. She wrote in one of her sprightly letters, "I belong at present neither to God nor the devil, and I find this condition very uncomfortable, though, between you and me, the most natural in the world." But nothing is really natural against which the nobler elements of our mixed nature lift a solemn remonstrance,—unheeded though it may be. If a heart could belong neither to this world nor the other there can at least be little doubt as to which is most likely to take possession. No levity, no deafness of disbelief, can silence the cry that forever sounds down to us from the heights, "Come out from among them, and be ye separate." That cry has two parts, equally commanding. If you have "come out," thank God and take courage! To keep yourself "separate" and "unspotted," demands a longer conflict, a stricter watch, a more patient and persistent and obedient determination to be "clean every whit."

"Thou passest by—Thy awful step I hear;
Thou passest by—Thy five dread wounds I see;
Thou passest by—Thy saving cross I clasp
With penitential tears of agony.

"Thou passest by—I will not let Thee go
Until Thy mercy streams into my soul;
I am sin-laden; lift the burden off,
For Thou alone canst heal and make me whole.

"Thou passest by—I pray to be illumed
With grace and light; so shall the darkness flee,
And these dim eyes, O Thou ascended Lord,
In rapture recognize and gaze on Thee!"

O GOD of hope, fill us, we beseech Thee, with all joy and peace in believing, and give to us ever-increasing strength in obedience, that abounding in hope through the power of the Holy Ghost we may steadily press on to those good things which Thou hast promised to those that shall endure to the end; through Jesus Christ our Lord. *Amen.*

First Saturday.

MASKS.

To make more vivid the spiritual conflict between the two opposite powers, the Master and His adversary, military images are multiplied. But there is a possibility of their misleading us. After they have been told of sword and shield, battle and blows, people shut their Bibles or go out of church, and see nothing of an enemy. Those martial metaphors, they say, must refer to some experience that they have never come to. What can they mean? This affluent estate, the palatial house, the superb furniture, the brilliant assembly, the merry feast, the eager traffic; they all look innocent enough, amiable, peaceable, friendly. There is no serpent's coil or tooth to be seen anywhere among the roses and wines. Why, this is the very flower of our civilization. This "Prince" that you would frighten us about brings in his train splendid gifts, handsome hospitalities, paintings and music, refinement and comfort. If he hates us and wants to destroy us, why does he not come with threat and challenge, with shot and bayonet, as warriors come? Ah, if he only would! Then we would be as brave as the bravest.

Take the more care. Watch with the keener vigilance. If the tempter can disguise himself as an angel of light, why not as a civilizer and educator, the benefactor and brightener of society? If he can gain your heart and hide God from you and make you a worshipper of yourself and turn you into a cultivated and polished animal, gliding in between the gift and the Giver, mixing the arsenic of death with the wine of life, addling your brain while he drugs your conscience with wicked elegance and indecent beauty, —why not? He knows his business. Half the battle is to see the adversary. The prayer of the Christian must be that of the Greek fighter, Give me light on the field! Do you pray that prayer? Do you pray it even in the Forty Days, "with strong crying and tears"?

Another snare lurks in the vagueness and generality of words, the very words we have been using here, words of warning and alarm. Everybody assents to the sharp text with a construction, to the sermon with an allowance for the professional phraseology. Men who intend to go on sinning put an accommodating sense into the boldest rebuke. The devil has a dictionary of his own. "The world, the flesh and the devil!" Why the pulpit has been ringing the changes on that name of the trinity of evil ever since the Gospel was preached. Let us not be alarmed! We will pay our pew tax, be civil to the clergy, and go our worldly ways as before! But where do the ways end?

There are some worshippers not so willingly deceived, not so meanly satisfied, seeking not indulgence in sin but escape from it and mastery over it, keeping a true Lent, sworn to the truth, lead where it will, followers of the One Master. Here and there is a soul that wants to face the whole law, afraid only of that hell that begins to burn in the guilty breast,—some prosperous man of business, who would not have his prosperity a disgrace or his house a mere hostelry to eat and drink and sleep in; some trader who holds his "talent" a trust to be multiplied and answered for; some inheritor of a large estate who feels that he is a steward under the Divine Owner, and is anxious to learn the duty of his stewardship; or here is a young man at the beginning of his career expecting success and thinking how to make it honorable, by uniting a manly use of his sagacity with an unostentatious consecration of his wealth to humanity and a steady preservation of what is most royal in his manhood; or here is a womanly woman, with time or money or power, too high-hearted and pure-hearted to live down to little aims or wasting dissipations. These persons are longing to ascend into a finer air. They have had enough of soft words and an outside piety. They will be glad of a fresh inspiration from the hills of God. There is a vision of those two contending kingdoms, and the practical question with them is how to live worthily. "There came one running to Jesus," rich and a ruler, "saying, What good thing shall I do that I may inherit eternal life?"

We need not spin out a very long answer. First, try to form an idea, for yourself, of what, for you, that besetting sin or forbidden thing is. Put one part of your Lord's teaching with another, study it, think about it, and make out an honest meaning. He knew God, eternity, His disciples' hearts, the worst of men and the best, the woman of Samaria and His mother, Pilate, the city, Herod's court, the Sanhedrim. He knew "the world" better than the most accomplished "man of the world" knows it. And, over and over again, out of His great love, He moves you and me to watch, to resist, to overcome—better yet, to see to it that the bad power, come when or how it will to us, finds nothing in us of its own. So speaks the whole New Testament. So does the Church all along. Find out what ways and doings, what talk and dress and indulgences in society hurt your spiritual life, or becloud your intercourse with God. Inquire how your treatment of any class or creature among your fellowmen compares with Christ's, your Master's, treatment of the poor servant, the publican, the Magdalen, Simon Peter, His tormentors. Call up one particular after another in this social life around you for judgment—not the people but the life, the prodigality, the pride, the contempt, the insincerity. Gradually you will see that the two kingdoms *are both there*, close by you; that there is a line between them; and you can find, if you will, where, for you at least, the line runs. Having found it, stand on the hither side of it, no matter what it costs, no matter what public opinion, sarcasm, fashion, all mankind may say. Keep the line sharp. Blurring it over is disobedience. Standing on the hither side, the Prince of the world will find nothing or less and less in you.

We find also that occupation with good is the best overcoming of evil. The way to keep the lower life out is to bring the higher life in, filling the soul with it up to the brim. Better than a constant skirmishing with the enemy down on his own level is an inward frame so full of Christ, so alive to noble inspirations, so busy about the Father's business, that temptation, when it comes, finds no door open. Christ was proof against the darkness because He was Himself the Light. Spread your feast, load your tables, O mammon, here is a Guest, coming in from heaven, who has meat to eat that your markets know not of—not fruit in baskets from any Sychar. You shall not live by bread only. Satan tries three times, and gives up, baffled, having nothing in that holy heart. Angels enter in, find room, and minister. The great souls we read of, their minds peopled with divine thoughts and clean affections, not dallying with things forbidden, just, patient, seeing God everywhere, standing well back from that border-line of iniquity—these not only overcome evil in the struggle, they overcome it with the good in them before it arrives.

The conflict is personal and private, seldom public. The public reform will come afterwards, little by little, in simplicity of manners, moderate amusements, high standards, lowly social pretentions, in charity, chastity, honesty. But think of others. Your personal lives touch one another and leave their mark. The acquaintance may be slight, the meetings few, but when all stand together at the last you will see that your own life lifted or lowered some forgotten lives about you. Think not only what you can safely do or afford in yourself, but what may tempt or embitter or corrupt those other souls, especially the young. When you say, in palliation of a dubious fashion, "To the pure all things are pure," consider mercifully that in every company there are hearts *not* pure, only struggling not to sink. Woe to you if you drag them down! "Evil to him who evil thinks," you say. It is a cold-blooded maxim. The "evil" is in you, and you are the Evil One's guilty minister if you so behave yourself that you start in man or woman evil thoughts. For there are unclean and low-lived things which are handsome to the eye, but which make it easier to live for ourselves, and the baser part of ourselves, harder to live on high with the "pure in heart" who "see God." Let the Prince come and let him go; let him sneer at your sacrifices and wonder at your satisfactions; let him gather up his purple and fine linen and leave you out of his receptions. For you there is the meat which he knows not of, and there are places prepared by the Master of the feast. An uncompromising conscience, a fearless faith, these are for you "the victory that overcometh the world." When the Prince cometh, looking in on that heart, he sees nothing of his own, and falls conquered at your feet.

"Our God, our Father, with us stay,
And make us keep Thy narrow way;
Free us from sin and all its power;
Give us a joyful dying hour;
Deliver us from Satan's arts,
And let us build our hopes on Thee,
Down in our very heart of hearts!
O God, may we true servants be,
And serve Thee ever perfectly.
Help us, with all Thy children here,
To fight and flee with holy fear;
Flee from temptation, and to fight
With Thine own weapons for the right;
Amen, amen, so let it be!
So shall we ever sing to Thee.
Hallelujah!"

WE entreat Thee, O God of all wisdom and Fountain of all goodness, that Thou wilt show us the right way, and incline us steadily and faithfully to walk in it. Engage all our powers and faculties in observing Thy commandments. Make our bodies fit temples for Thy Holy Spirit to dwell in, so that, with temperance and purity, all our desires and appetites may be subdued to Thine incorruptible will, and no excess or sloth darken our minds or deaden our consciences. Teach us to prize honor more than comfort, and usefulness to our fellow-men more than their favor. Lift us above a weak or wicked fear of human opinions. Set us free from foolish fashions and wrong customs. Restrain us from following any multitude to do evil. Grant us patience whenever we are provoked, courage when we are ready to despair, and perseverance unto the end. May nothing ever seem too hard for us to do, or to suffer, in following Him, our crucified and glorified Master, who bore the cross and laid down His life for us. And this we beg in the name of Him, our Redeemer, who, with Thee and the Holy Ghost, liveth and reigneth, one God, world without end. *Amen.*

First Monday.

THE CREATION TRAVAILING IN PAIN.

EVEN in the natural material world, a great army of physical maladies come against us, and are too much for us. We are not equal to these mighty forces in the earth. Severities of climate, flood and fire, the malaria in the air—they harm, they drown, they poison us. Experience, science, books and doctors help us a little; but when they have done their best we know not much more about the causes of things in the universe we live in than children sporting in the palace-yard know of the counsels of the royal court within. Years of toil bring one a few handfuls from the boundless wealth of land and sea. We call it property, use a part of it rather awkwardly a little while, wish we had more, mourn over what we have, and succumb to death.

Accidents mangle us. Our friends and helpers look on helpless. Not being masters of Nature we are weary striving with her; and not being her innocent children we are never at rest on her bosom. In fact, in Nature there is for man no such thing as rest; there is no Heaven in man's natural life. The whole creation groaneth and travaileth in pain together, restlessly waiting for the manifestation of the serene son of God.

It is so also in the social world. Look from the outside at almost any party of pleasure. The surface is a sea of sunshine, waves of song and laughter rippling over it. But underneath there are dismal abysses of anxiety, tortures of disappointment and disquiet. The guests are afraid of one another, and the host is afraid of the guests, and the most are wondering whether they have held their own and done their best. It is because there are not personal resources enough to make success sure. Intellectually we are like the blind man by the roadside, wishing our eyes might be opened, seeing only glimpses of light, and reading only margins of the mysterious page. Physically, we are like the lame man at the Temple gate, begging not of Apostles but of the apothecary, of the physician, of the seashore, of the mountains. Morally, we are like the publican or the woman at Simon's table, only that we are too often less blessed than they because without their humility and tears. Yes, the Lord knew! It is weary work and weary play; striving, complaining, calculating, clutching, and failing after all. Who tells you he has succeeded? As pitiful a document as I ever read in my life was the private letter of one of the two or three most brilliant and most honored statesmen that this whole nation has ever known, declaring his whole course a mortifying disappointment, and saying he could look with composure on only two hiding-places,—a lonely chateau in some secluded valley of Switzerland, or a grave at Mount Auburn. More celebrity, more compliments, a higher office, finer pageants, a showier style! You "labor" for them; you are "heavy laden" with care or pride if you get them; you are "heavy laden" with vexation and envy if you do not. Did not the Master *know* the heart He spoke to, and the world He came to save? Come unto Me from the market-places, and the mountains, and the sea; from the crowds and the solitudes; from the public strife and shame of the nation; from secret fear and grief; from broken cisterns that can hold no water,—Come, and in my Life, in my Faith, my Hope, my Charity, in Me, your soul shall rest.

These are only illustrations, and we must come

down to the one real root of all the misery. The inward world shapes and makes the outer one. If it were not for sin, life would be, if not a perpetual victory, at least easy. Desire and attainment would be equal. All those bitter and countless kinds of wretchedness which come of evil within, unkindness, injustice, lust, intemperance, disobedience, cruelty, idleness, every vice and every crime would disappear. They all came in when Nature failed at the Fall; and nothing but a new order, redemption, can heal them. It requires the one cross of infinite sharpness and heaviness to lighten all the million million crosses that agonize the sinning race.

Look back a moment to the Garden in Genesis. There was nothing of what we now call labor. There was service going on. Adam was not idle in Eden. "The Lord God put him into the garden, to dress it and to keep it." But the work was not greater than the workman's power.

"To prune these growing plants and tend these flowers,"

Milton writes,—

"No more toil
Of their sweet gardening-labor then sufficed
To recommend cool zephyrs and made ease
More easy, wholesome thirst and appetite."

The "sweat of the brow," symbol of suffering and curse of transgression, was not yet. Instead of the fret and friction of excessive tasks, everything was done in a style of liberty. It was perpetual recreation, easy as to breathe and exhilarating as a game. The world without and the world within were in harmony. Transgression broke everything into confusion. The very materials wrought upon became tough and obstinate. Things presented their rough edges and wrong ends first. "Thorns also and thistles," just as God predicted, "the earth brought forth;" but then the thistle-seed and the sting of the thorn were first in the guilty soul. Men and women had to learn what hardship and lack of sympathy and a thousand other living sacrifices are, labor that is labor, burdens that are burdens. And then began the long human sigh for "rest." Then began the prophetic promise,—"There remaineth a rest,"—Sabbatismos—"for the people of God." Far off at Bethlehem, the "Seed of the woman," born in a mortal mother's pain, despised and rejected, dying in the torments of crucifixion, must "bruise the serpent's head." In himself man was no longer equal to his original destiny. He fell from it a fractured, disordered, heavy-laden creature, never to rise but as he should be lifted from above through faith in his Deliverer. The sting of death, the sting of birth, the sting of sick-beds, of business and failure in business, and of all mortal life is sin. To see what ought to be done, and not to do it,—to feel what a perfect life of love would be, and not to live it,—is not this the bitterness of a crippled and yet an aspiring will?

The old Bible words are law and transgression. What ought to be done is the law; our not doing it is the transgression. Through that rent in God's order have crept in all the downfalls of mankind. You read St. Paul's marvellously vivid description of the unsuccessful struggle of man's conscience to keep God's commandment, and it is the story of your failure. The more law you get, if law is all you get, the more infirmity comes to light. To speak of rest is mockery. All along through the Prophets runs the minor music of this majestic lamentation. Many of the Psalms are a *Miserere* over it. Hebrew history is a kind of wailing cry all through. "I cannot save myself; who shall deliver me? I am dying; who shall give me life? I see goodness, and it is divinely beautiful; but in the very light of it I see that I am not good." For any man, for you, for me, there is no labor, no burden like this. Give man rest from that, and you will give him salvation, and put the song of everlasting life upon his lips. Christ descended into a whole creation groaning and travailing with this burden, and amidst its awful helplessness and despair uttered His gracious and masterful word of mercy, "Come unto me, and this long, deadly conflict shall end. Take My forgiveness, and choose My eternal Life, and this will give you rest."

"No good
Or glory of this life but comes by pain.
How poor were earth in all its martyrdoms,
If all its struggling sighs of sacrifice
Were swept away, and all were satiate—smooth;
If this were such a heaven of soul and sense
As some have dreamed of; and we human still.
Nay, we were fashioned not for perfect peace
In this world, howsoever in the next;
And what we win and hold is through some strife."

O MOST Merciful Lord, who hast pity on the pain of the whole creation, who healest the inward man by outward afflictions, and who, by troubles in this world, dost prepare us for eternal joys, by that cup of sorrow which Thou drankest for us, and by that weary path which Thou troddest, grant that we may willingly drink of Thy cup and cheerfully follow Thee along the road where Thou hast gone before. Thou who with Father and the Holy Ghost livest and reignest one God, world without end. *Amen.*

First Tuesday.

MAN AND THE SON OF MAN.

In His dealings with persons what Christ really deals with is what we all have, carry about with us, take to church, keep Fasts and Feasts with, live and die with ;—we call it human nature. The characteristics of the persons are the differentials; beneath them is the common stock of humanity, with all its traits, capacities, possibilities of glory and of shame ; and so these persons, however various, are never very far from us. It is, in this way, His apparently casual and undesigned meetings with individuals that bring out before the world and the ages many of the most momentous revelations, most original principles, and most comprehensive verities of His religion and His kingdom.

There was a signal instance of this wonderful, swift transition from insignificant particulars to universal truth at the well-side in Samaria. At that out-of-the-way halting-place the Master found this common human nature, reached after it, searched it out in a woman, as at other times He found it in men. She was an unpromising specimen of her kind, volatile, immodest, her mind cramped by the prejudices of a petty province, her habits sunk in the frivolities of her own sex and the sensuality of the other. Her name is delicately concealed. Christ takes her as He finds her, just as He always does, and just as the Gospel of His grace and power always will, takes her not for what she *is*, but for what she can be, not because she is agreeable or deserving, but because, though disagreeable, she is in peril; and, being undeserving, her Lord pities her the more, and will save her if she will consent to be saved. It will be equal to the most splendid of his miracles if a soul so dark and defiled can be lifted up into the light of faith, into the honor of chastity, into the peace that passeth understanding, into the holy freedom of a daughter of God. From that day down to this, this miracle has been wrought, wherever this Traveller through Samaria has come, out to the ends of the earth.

See how simple the Master's way is. First, He has this human nature in Himself, the same that is in every flighty woman, every profane man. Never was there so much of this common humanity in any one born of a woman as in this Jesus of the Galilean carpenter's shop, this manliest of men, who, therefore, loved to call Himself "Son of Man;" whose hunger, and blood, and tears are ours, but whose life, and love, and saving power are God's alone; "in whom dwelleth all the fulness of God bodily." Understand thoroughly that except for this perfect oneness of heart between the sinner and the Saviour there would have been no such divine story told, and no salvation possible. We never make out to help one another much in our deepest troubles without this mutual recognition, which seems to say, by look, or tone, or some nameless sign, "You and I are made of the same stuff; we are hurt and we are healed, we ache and we are tempted, we go wrong and get scourged or comforted in the same way." You may help your neighbor by the smaller benefits of your money, your custom, your vote, or your advice, without much of this common feeling; but the heart in its deeper pain you will never reach—its heavier grief its untold tragedy, its lonely heartache, and the bitter sense of wrong—without the fellow-sense which makes mankind a brotherhood. We live a common life; heart answers to heart; the lost are found by love; sin is conquered by a cross; and only by "the *Man Christ Jesus*" are men redeemed. "The woman left her water-pot" lying by the well, "and went her way into the city, and saith to the men," with a manner they had never seen in her before, "Come, see a man which told me all things that ever I did. Is not this the Christ?" It will take a great many modern skeptics, however much they may fancy they know, to tear out of the world's heart, or wrench out of its hand, a Book full of human realities like this.

Enter farther into the meaning of the Lord's treatment of that wayward soul. It stands out an example of the strong grasp of His religion on mankind. More than that, it shows us how by Him the kingdom of heaven may come into our own lives, to sweeten and glorify them, and how you and I, no matter what we may have been hitherto, may be, if we will, sons and daughters of God. In other words, it opens the magnificent mystery of salvation.

What are the two materials that the Master uses in this grand object-lesson of our spiritual life? Two very plain, familiar, commonplace things—a daily sensation of our bodies, and a free bounty out of the heart of the earth,—thirst and water. Suppose a preacher of our day were about to preach his most original and profoundest sermon, proclaiming to the world a message which four thousand years of prophets and priests had been longing to utter—royal prophets, like Isaiah and David; superb high-priests, like Aaron and Hilkiah—would he not have kept his remarkable discourse for some rare occasion, a university audience of scholars, or an upper-class throng in a metropolitan church? Two such deep questions were now to be answered once for all, questions that these prophets and priests had been asking anxiously of each other, asking of the hills and the stars, ever since Eli watched all night in the temple, ever since the patriarch, in the rocky pasture, leaning on the top of his staff, looked up into the midnight sky, his children and his cattle lying asleep around him in their tents, while he hearkened for the voice of God,—two questions: Wherewith shall a man come before his Maker, a sinning man before his sinless Maker? or, what is worship? How shall an accusing conscience find rest? or what is reconciliation? Christ answers them both. He takes a rustic well-stone for His pulpit, and for His audience one light-minded water-carrier, and for His illustrations the pitcher in her hand and Mt. Gerizim rising southward, crowned with the noonday light; and for His sermon two sentences: "We know what we worship; God is a Spirit, and they that worship Him must worship Him in spirit and in truth." That is one answer. It clears the ground for the Christian Church, on a new earth, under new heavens. "Whosoever drinketh of this water shall thirst again; but whosoever drinketh of the water that I shall give him shall never thirst; it shall be a well of water springing in him into everlasting life, the gift of God." This is the other. It opens the kingdom of God to all believers, of every climate and every age. It will be wise for us, heavenly wisdom, to ponder these two sayings a while in silence, in secrecy, placing ourselves there by the well, before we run away from ourselves, and from them, and from Him who spoke them, to seek human interpretations of them from other interpreters.

"Thou knowest, Lord, the weariness and sorrow
 Of the sad heart that comes to Thee for rest;
Cares of to-day and burdens for to-morrow,
 Blessings implored, and sins to be confessed.
I come before Thee, at Thy gracious word,
And lay them at Thy feet: Thou knowest, Lord!

"Thou knowest not alone as God all-knowing:
As *man* our mortal weakness Thou hast proved;
On earth, with purest sympathies o'erflowing,
O Saviour, Thou hast wept, and Thou hast loved!
And love and sorrow still to Thee may come,
And find a hiding-place, a rest, a home.

"Therefore I come, Thy gentle call obeying,
And lay my sins and sorrows at Thy feet,
On everlasting strength my weakness staying,
Clothed in Thy robe of righteousness complete:
Then rising and refreshed I leave Thy throne,
And follow on, to know as I am known."

O CHRIST our God, Who wilt come to judge the world in the Manhood which Thou hast assumed, we pray Thee to sanctify us wholly, that in the day of Thy Coming our whole spirit, soul and body may so revive to a fresh life in Thee that we may live and reign with Thee forever. *Amen.*

Second Wednesday.

THE MASTER THE CONQUEROR.

In warfare the first condition of victory is to know the enemy, to know him well enough, at the least, to distinguish him from a friend. The more distinct and accurate this knowledge of the enemy is, as to his whereabouts, habits, disposition, tactics, objects, the greater the likelihood of success, whether in defence or attack. The Christian life is not all warfare, but it is warfare. No man or woman ever lived it without finding that out. There are other things to be done besides fighting,—building, planting, tilling, serving, healing, receiving light and giving light, adding to the life and giving it to others. From beginning to end the process is twofold, positive and negative, gaining and resisting, extending truth by love, and overcoming hostility. We not only learn this by experience; the military imagery runs all through Gospels and Epistles; the Master illustrates His Gospel of glory and good-will by it; we sing it in our hymns. These all call the enemy "the world."

They are too much in earnest, too intent and intense in purpose, too luminously inspired, too complete in their understanding of what is to be done, to use language loosely or indefinitely. They are not much given to definition, but in one way or another they are apt to make us comprehend what they mean, and see what we are to believe and do, what we are to believe and why, what we are to do and how. We need not go beyond our Lord's own words. He makes the antagonism manifest, complete, deadly. "I am not of the world." "The world hateth me, and hateth you." "I have overcome the world." "The Prince of this world cometh and hath nothing in me." St. John insists upon it with an agony of anxiety and alarm. Our eternal life is in incessant and terrible danger from "the world." Lent is granted to make us strong, steadfast, watchful, keen-sighted, patient, and victorious in the contest.

If the spirit of docility and loyal soldiership is in us we shall not quibble or cavil much as to what "the world" is. There is not much room for honest mistake. We all know well enough that it is not this visible frame of material things which

God has made, and made in beauty and grandeur, blessing it, and pronouncing it "very good." Nor is it the world of lawful business, of wholesome enterprise, of moderate recreation, of artistic delight. It would be a stupid affectation to pretend not to know what worldliness is in the heart or the life of man or woman. It is the sum of unspiritual forces, ungodly passions, the ambitions, appetites, competitions, indulgences, entertainments, in which self prevails, rules, reigns uncontrolled. We are supposed to be at our Master's feet, near His cross, listening to Him.

When He says, "The prince of this world cometh, and hath nothing in Me," He might have said, "I am going out to fight the prince of this world, and shall conquer him." The meaning might seem, at first sight, to be the same, but there is a remarkable difference. In the latter phrase the consciousness of power would be extraordinary, but the moral majesty would be less. In the other He tell us not only that He is a conqueror, but what kind of power He conquers by. It is not a larger quantity of the same kind of power that makes "the world" powerful, but a power of a different quality and nature. He says it is "in Me." It is inward power then. Not by sword, and shot, and club, and battle-axe, but by the silent strength of an incorruptible heart, by the irresistible front of conscience and will, by the majestic superiority of character, He wins and prevails. As with the Master, so with every one of His true followers. Two principles of human life and conduct are crowding for admittance at the door of the soul. As far as one comes in the other must stand back in any heart, any family, any society, any age. You cannot always distinguish them by the scenes where they appear, the instruments and weapons they use, the clothes they wear; and sometimes you can. But each of the two is sure to work itself out and manifest itself at last in a whole array of visible things, in manners, fashions, furniture, signs of the ruling principle within. Both have been contending actively with each other since the first man and woman were tempted. They are such that we cannot by any caution keep ourselves out of the conflict, or be on both sides at once. We may try to; we may imagine that we do, deceiving ourselves and one another. It is not of the least use. History may divide mankind by races; geography by countries. But the dividing line between Hindoo and Saxon, between sea and land, between a purple mountain and a pale sky, is not half so deep or so indelible as this. Christ calls the two sorts two kingdoms, which means more than mere feelings, sentiments, or opinions. Each kingdom has one of two principles at its root, and the same roots are in every human breast. You personally are in one of the two kingdoms. Public signals are put out, as each works by its own will and law; on one side are adoring worshippers, great charities, holy fasts and feasts, anthems of praise, penitential prayers, these Forty Days, sacraments, Christian hospitals, reformatories, schools, signs of the kingdom of Christ the Conqueror; on the other you see luxurious living, unprincipled display, unscrupulous politics, unclean play-houses, tempting and seductive dress, lotteries, gambling-houses, secularism taking the name and mark of religion, a shameless press. But you look closer and see that these external signs are not always accurate, because the children of "the world" get sometimes on to the ground and into the company of the Church. Yet you may be sure, nevertheless, that the principles are two, only two, that the two roots of life are there, that the line runs between them. What an awful certainty it is! One is self, in one of its three forms—self-indulgence, self-promotion, self-will—de termined to have its own way, by hands or brain, by force or calculation, by money or craft, by seduction, by lying, by class-privileges, by extravagances that belittle other people's fortunes, or rouse other people's envy, gratifying appetite or vanity. The other principle is unselfish love for God and for men because they are men and God's children, making its way by disinterested kindness, by dealings of unyielding integrity and unspotted honor, by willing sacrifice, by truth fearlessly told in all companies and at all costs, by gentle judgments, by discarding utterly and instantly in every question the narrow bounds of prejudice or pride, by the glory of character, by doing God's will, by likeness to the Son of Man. This is the antagonist of worldliness. You cannot stigmatize it as "other worldliness," for every feature of it is belonging, and working, and triumphing, in this world where we live. It is unworldliness, but it is more; it is the kingdom of God and heaven on the earth.

This is what Christ meant. This is what was in His mind, not only in the Forty Days, but all the time. His life and death, His Gospel and cross, His resurrection and ascension, signify nothing less. He sets the two kingdoms over against one another, by setting His own up among men in the living form of a perfect, inextinguishable life. The world's men hate Him because He is not of them. The prince of them comes, looks at Him, and has nothing in Him. Against that prince and his host He sends out no army, with trumpets, banners, swords. If His kingdom were of this world then would His servants fight. It is the brotherhood of men under the Fatherhood of God, and fighting is no part of its business. It is love, truth, righteousness in the souls of His people.

So He matches Himself against "the world." Let it come! Let it do its worst, by temptation, by flattery, by bribes, by pomps and pageants, by seduction, by terrors. Nothing in Him answers to it, mixes with it, wants it, yields it a foothold, can be bought by it, or terrified by it. Without a blow from His hand or a curse from His tongue it falls helpless at His feet. However it looks, whoever leads society, whatever the season's gaiety or glamour, the piling up of property, the illusions, the boasts, the lies, the Master is King to the end of time, the world is overcome, and every one of the world's sons and daughters will know it in the end.

"'The world against me; I against the world.'
Strange words for him* who just now stood
On Alexandria's throne, and hurled
His thunders as he would!
What loneliness this outer strength doth hide
What longing lies beneath this calm!
For human sympathy this great heart cried,
Our earth's divinest balm.

"But more than sympathy my trust I prize,
Above my friendships hold I God,
Bound, banished be their feet, ere they despise
The path their Master trod.
So let my banner be again unfurled,
Again its fearless watchword seen,
'The world against me, I against the world,'
Judge Thou, O Christ, between!"

ALMIGHTY and everlasting God, Who hast revealed Thy glory, by Christ, among all nations, preserve the works of Thy mercy; that Thy Church, which is spread throughout the world, may persevere with steadfast faith in the confession of Thy Name; through Jesus Christ our Lord. *Amen.*

---

* St. Athanasius.

Second Thursday.

WHO CAN BE SAVED?

SALVATION is a state of personal spiritual health before God. It is not a single act, or a place; though it begins with an action, and there is always a place for it and for those who have it. It belongs to us—not complete, but growing in us—wherever we may be. The habit of putting it off is a habit of those who really do not want it. A habit of preaching it as if it could be had only after death, and in another world, comes of a mistaken idea of what it is, a misunderstanding of some parts of the Bible-language, and learning theology from modern Scribes rather than from Him who saves us. They think of it as a private possession, not as a character; as what a man may get rather than what he is; as an escape from harm, not a life, in these streets and houses, of holy liberty and royal fellowship with strong and righteous spirits of all ages. A Christian gentleman who spent his strength and fortune working and praying with intense energy and a cheerful temper for the lost was asked by one of these blind leaders whether he had a hope of being saved. He answered reverently that as he was busy trying to save his neighbors in obedience to a Saviour whom he loved and trusted, the question whether he would be saved at a future time had not occupied him.

Whatever else salvation may be, it is not a private property; still less is it a class privilege. Christian salvation has been preached to fifty generations. Two mistakes about it—first a misconception and then a misrepresentation—have been subtle and pernicious, fearfully limiting its power. One is that Christ saves the individual from discomfort or hardship, which is precisely what He did not come into the world to do; the other that before men can be saved they must be favored with an intellectual comprehension of religious mysteries, and have facts and commands which are presented to one of their capacities, their faith, explained to another and smaller capacity, the understanding, which Christ over and over again declares not to be true. Religious performances gone through to ward off a fiery trouble by and by may be a safe economy, but they are not Christianity, any more than it would be Christianity for a strong man to run out of a house on fire, leaving invalids and children there to burn. He saves his body, but *he* is not saved. So if I, being ordered to preach the Gospel, call upon you to master certain theological systems, or verify certain scientific speculations, instead of taking facts revealed with a child's faith and living upon them a devout and righteous life, then I am no more a prophet of God than Isaiah would have been if he had told Israel to give up idolatry because it injured their political prosperity; or Jonah if he had exhorted the Ninevites to run away from the doomed city instead of repenting of their sins; or St. Paul if he had reasoned with the Ephesians that they would earn better wages by making ornaments for Christian churches than by making silver shrines for Diana; or St. John if he had turned rationalist and written, "This is the victory that overcometh the world, even your 'education.'" Salvation is holy character, not intellectual but spiritual. It is by the grace of God. Salvation is taking the lowest place, if that will save other men for Christ's sake. Salvation is such a penetrating sense of personal unworthiness as obliges you to make an honest confession to God and a hearty prayer for pardon. Salvation is giving up what we like and denying ourselves what is wrong from the same motive that Christ did—from charity. Salvation is choosing to be like Christ rather than be popular or prosperous. Plainly, as you see, it is not a private property, or a fruit of culture, or a product of schools and universities, or a class privilege.

A "common salvation," then, is not an inferior or second-rate sort of salvation. In New Testament speech, as in our English tongue, the word "common," has two meanings. In one sense it is a term of disparagement. In that sense a "common" thing is a cheap or vulgar thing, without sanctity or dignity. Common meat St. Peter refused to eat till it was made sacred. Common hands were unwashed hands. But elsewhere what is common is what belongs to the larger number and is the more worthy portion, like sunlight or water, like the *common* wealth, *common* sense, the Book of *Common* Prayer, a *common* life. St. Paul reminds Titus that, though working apart, they both have a "common faith." Why is it a proof of divine power in Christ that the "*common* people" were glad to hear Him? Because the *un*common people, Scribes, Pharisees and office-holders,—*i. e.*, the arrogant and conceited literary class, the bigoted religious class, and the lying political class, who all expected an *un*common or exclusive salvation—fell under His rebuke, were seen through and exposed in their varnished but inbred vulgarity. It was they who were second-best. Christ knew it, and they knew that He knew it, and they felt towards Him as tyrants and charlatans always feel towards true prophets; they feared Him, hated Him, and would crucify Him if they could. Why were the common people any better, having less knowledge, less property, less reputation? Not certainly because they were ignorant, poor or unknown. That is the flattering falsehood of demagogues, told to purchase or please a party, with no honor or religion in it. Nor are common people the better for being in a majority. Saints or heroes are rarely found there. Their advantage is simply that there is more in them of essential and unmixed humanity as God made it, less corrupted by wealth, luxury and ambition. This was true of the divine Workman of Nazareth. Human nature in Him, not as to its corruption, but as to its natural wholesomeness, was abundant, unspoilt, open and free. He and the people were one, understanding each other because feeling alike. Was it not known that He was brought up in the shop of a carpenter, and was never in the colleges of the rabbis? The title He chose for Himself was "Son of Man." What the world wanted was God in man. You and I, so far as our humanity is not eaten out, have something in us common to us and Jesus of Nazareth, our Lord, who becomes in this way a common Saviour by a common salvation.

"No, no! the energy of life may be
Kept on after the grave, but not begun!
And he who flagged not in the earthly strife,
From strength to strength advancing—only he,
His soul well-knit and all his battles won,
Mounts, and that hardly, to eternal life"

WE adore Thee, blessed Jesus, very God and very man, the same yesterday, to-day, and for ever, our strong Salvation, and our only Hope. Take us, we pray Thee, into Thy keeping, both now, and at the hour of our death; make us faithful to Thee upon earth, and blessed with Thee in heaven, where with the Father and the Holy Ghost, Thou livest and reignest, ever one God, world without end. *Amen.*

Second Friday.

HOW CHRISTIANS MAY NOT BE SAVED.

A MISCONCEPTION of the nature of salvation leads very directly to a misconception of the way of salvation.

Here. very largely, is what is the matter with the Church now. It is our disease, our impotence. What we lack is faith in the commonness or simplicity of the Faith. You will not deny that something ails our religious condition. Measure the Church in this country as it is by the New Testament, by the Epistle to the Ephesians, by the Sermon on the Mount, by its Prayer Book, by its professions of Evangelic Truth and Apostolic Order, by its intelligence, by its wealth even,—and you will have to confess that it is small and imbecile, sordid and cowardly, mean-spirited, self-occupied and worldly-minded. Lay the measuring-line down closer on your own Christian household and economy, for time is too short for anything but searching honesty. Ought not years of such worship, such Scriptures, such sacraments and such sermons as you have had, to have reared a sturdier piety, to have spread abroad a wider and deeper sanctity, and put out a stronger evangelizing power into the neighborhood about you? We would not willingly let our style of Christianity be set up as the standard for mankind. Salvation we have had, over and over, in hymns, and sermons without number. But though harvests are past and summers ended we are not saved yet with a grand and glorious,—no, nor with any safe salvation.

And this is owing to our shallow and shrunk idea of the common faith. Men come to tell you earnestly enough and with plausible explanations that the difficulty is unbelief in this or that particular doctrine, and they go painfully about by elaborate reasonings to convince the people's understanding that there is a God, that the universe had a Maker, that a chapter in Genesis is accurate as to its geology, and to beg that the Book which has created Christendom and bowed the highest heads of eighteen centuries in reverent adoration may be forbearingly handled by modern college professors and literary lecturers. They expect to lead men into the Kingdom of Heaven by an argument. They hope to awaken spiritual life by rational ingenuity, to make sinning and tempted men and frivolous women to be holy-hearted and humble-hearted and pure-hearted, by making them keen-sighted, to get them down on their knees in repentance, or to enrapture them with the splendor in the face of Christ and the beauty of His Beatitudes, by clearing up a metaphysical puzzle or an ecclesiastical scruple or a grammatical paradox in the praises of saints to whom the heavens were opened. Our Lord Himself certainly did not take that way. Yet He knew all that is in man, and all that is not in man, all that is in earth and all that is in Heaven. He and the Apostles He sent gave not a particle of encouragement to the notion that sinners are to find a path into the Kingdom of Heaven by their wits. They were prompt and clear in declaring that there are blessed things which "pass man's understanding"—better, higher, deeper, grander things,—the *love* of God that passeth knowledge, the *peace* of God that passeth *all* understanding, the realities which the princes and wise men of this world never knew, but realities nevertheless, certain, and certain to be known hereafter, and held fast meantime by faith. There has been quite attention enough paid to the intellectual difficulties of a few fastidious skeptics. Doubts that are constitutional or irresistible are to be handled with pity and pains by those who are competent,—as Christ handled the doubts of Thomas. But the noisy doubters that we hear most, or most about, need converting more than they need convincing. The atheists need less to be told that there is a God than to see what kind of a God God is. And if few are saved, it is a good deal because salvation is not taken as a noble gift to be had on simple terms, and by that gift of grace to be a steady growth in us, till, gradually in a perfecting of Christian manhood and womanhood, we come to the measure of the stature of the fulness of Christ.

For every soul that is lost outside the Church by atheism, a thousand perish within the Church by an impious complacency, fancying that they are Christ's disciples because of their manners, their education, their social standing, or their ceremonial decency. When one thinks of the parables of Christ, of the divine morality of the Epistles, of the cross, of the later chapters of St. John, and then of the Scribe who is the type of a host of modern scholars, and the Pharisee who is a type of a larger host of modern communicants, and then of the Last Judgment, there is hardly a more alarming spectacle, I think, than one of our fashionably-clad congregations. Were one of these Simons to entertain the Lord Jesus at his table, and were the woman out of the street to creep in, we should hear again the question, "Which of them loves him most?" and again the voice of the common Master, "Thy faith hath saved thee, Go in peace;"—the common faith bringing in the common salvation.

Ages ago, in a famine of heavenly bread, amid the dry repetition of barren formalities in a temple emptied of its spiritual refreshments, in a Church where the self-conceit of Scribes had killed both penitence and faith, there came the cry of a hungry heart, "Wherewith shall I come before the Lord?" We here keep, or pretend to keep, not Hebrew Sabbaths but Lord's Days, feasts where Christ gives food and drink. As we enter the door, and move towards the altar, and shut our eyes, and pretend to pray, how many of us inwardly ask that question? "Wherewith shall I come?" What is the offering we bring? It is not a great deal that God asks. He asks that we want Him, asks that we mean what we say, asks that we are ready to take what we come for, a common salvation; that in His house we will not be hypocrites, self-satisfied and willing to seem better than we are, but Prodigals and Magdalens,—Prodigals, lost in pride, not in sottish sensuality perhaps, but in self-will, self-indulgence, self-admiration; Magdalens,—not of the street, but of vanity, and envying, and imaginations which we should not dare to lay open; prodigals and Magdalens by passions which respectability, not the fear or love of God, holds in check.

One thing is certain, because the law is fixed. What you do not come for you will not carry away. If you come for the exercise or diversion of a curious or restless mind, you will not find spiritual help, light or strength. Temptation will be as dangerous as ever, and your character as faulty, *plus* the guilt of a false pretence. Coming to church for a Sunday decency you will have had a decent Sunday. "Verily they have their reward." Coming to get something from man and nothing from God, the distance between you and God will be widened. No man is great before God on account of his opinions. Coming with no humble sense that you need first of all to be forgiven, making no sincere confession, with nothing childlike in your heart, you are among the fools who make a mock at sin. Men do not gather grapes of thorns, or righteousness of a picturesque function in a chancel, or a tender conscience by criticising choir or sermon. "Stand in the gate of the Lord's House, and listen. Hear the word of the Lord, all ye that enter in at these gates to worship. Trust ye not in lying words, saying, The Temple of the Lord, the Temple of the Lord, the Temple of the Lord, are we. Amend your ways and your doings; execute justice between a man and his neighbor; hurt not the stranger, the fatherless or the widow. Worship no false God,"—or ye shall call and there shall be no answer.

These are warnings. For every warning there is a promise. Warning and promise are not to be taken apart in any message from God. God's promises exceed all that we can desire. So do His reckonings exceed all that we can dread. No man ever found the way of salvation, common and open as it is, who did not see that there is a way of danger. And yet, as the Gospel tidings are "glad," as the news is "good news," as God is Love, and duty is delightful, and Heaven is the land of beauty indescribable lying "far up the Everlasting hills," "in God's own light," we ought to part and go away with the promise: "Whosoever will, let him come." "Him that cometh to me I will in no wise cast out."

"No word of doom may shut thee out,
No word of wrath may downward whirl,
No swords of fire keep watch about
The open gates of pearl.
Forever round the mercy-seat
The guiding lights of Love shall burn.
But what if habit-bound thy feet
Shall lack the will to turn?"

O RIGHTEOUS and merciful God, look favorably upon the people, we beseech Thee, and bestow upon us Thy continual grace; that assisted by Thy power and comfort here we may omit nothing necessary to our Salvation, but strive ever more earnestly towards everlasting blessedness; through Christ our Lord. *Amen.*

Second Saturday.

HOW CHRISTIANS MAY BE SAVED.

WHEN we know what salvation is, we have an easy path into the central doctrine in the Creed of the Church. Its theological name is the Incarnation. Its name in every-day language would be God in man, God on earth among human families and employments. Men having got apart from God by putting their appetites, business and amusements in the first and highest place forgot what kind of a God He is. Various devices for bringing heaven and earth together failed,—because they were all outside of the man—a splendid ritual, "the law," a national polity. But what if God should take up what is in us into Himself, and live out before our eyes perfect goodness, perfect wisdom and strength and sacrifice, in a woman's son? That would be the want met, the hunger filled, the hurt healed, the Father coming out to meet the lost child a great way off, sin forgiven and life everlasting made certain. See what this Christian manhood was, not Jewish, or Asiatic, or European, or African, or American humanity, but humanity pure and simple, absolute, universal, "common." You notice that in all countries, all climates, and all ranks, the Christian is the same kind of man, a growth of one stock. You recognize the stamp everywhere under all types and colors and degrees of cultivation, and you say, That man, that woman, is of Christ. Christ creates the type. His religion, His life, fits every nationality alike. It adapts and applies itself graciously, too, as a saving force, to every part of us as we are made; the reason, the will, affection, imagination,—every sensibility to joy or grief, every fibre of the flesh, every period, interest, pursuit of life. It is catholic to the individual constitution as to the race; out of this one fountain-life, in a new creation by a second Adam, flow all the streams that water and fertilize and sweeten the four quarters of the earth:

> "See the rivers four that gladden
> With their streams the better Eden
> Planted by our Lord most dear.
> Christ the Fountain, these the waters,
> Drink, O Ziön's sons and daughters,
> Drink and find salvation here.'

Out of Him history begins again, itself regenerated. Out of Him grows the living, spreading, healing Tree.

Now we know what catholicity means and how and why the Church is catholic. Out of the common Christ come all its gifts of the Spirit, all sacramental helps, washing, nourishment; out of Him the creed that never changes; out of Him the voices that sound the good news from land to land, from age to age; the feet beautiful upon the mountains east and west, the martyrs in robes of fire, the million-fold confessions of all living and dying saints, the flocks that worship by the Ganges to-day, and your neighbor who died with the common Name on His lips last night, the whole multitude that no man can number in the city that lies four square, with gates open on all the sides.

See this commonness in the fact that, from first to last in His life, Christ kept Himself at the bottom of society. If Jesus had been born and bred in any one of what we call the "upper classes," then the lower classes, plebeians and peasants and slaves, might have distrusted His sympathy and rejected His condescension. Had He been a companion of the rich, or lodged in a mansion, had He borne the titles of a university or an earthly nobility, then forlorn and homeless hearts might have asked, what does this child of comfort know about us, our poverty, our hardships, our bondage, our loneliness? But of Him who was poorer than the bird in its nest or the fox in his hole no pauper or outcast or toilsman in the cotton-field or the factory or the city streets can say that. Between the manger and the cross there was wrought out, for you and me, a "common salvation."

This is much more than a general, abstract truth. This spiritual quality of our religion—which is a glory of it—is not set up here as a mere historical curiosity, a striking phenomenon which marks a distinction between the Christian and other systems of religious belief. I am not presenting it to you at all as if you were students or critics or judges, but exactly the contrary. It is a matter of the closest personal concern. What the way of salvation is for the world at large is one question. But what is it to you? We get into a habit of treating God's message as we do the topics of the day, the books we read, the languages or sciences we learn. It becomes, *i. e.*, a thing for the mind to deal with, a thing to be looked at, talked about, debated, reported in the newspapers agitated in conventions, analyzed and recommended in sermons. This is a part of the exaggerated, one-sided importance given, in these days, to the workings and speculations of one faculty in us which we flatter by calling it intellectual, but which yields by no means the richest or deepest or sweetest satisfactions of our life. It is a radical, terrible, disastrous mistake. Nobody here is so blind or so lunatic as to discredit the solid contributions of knowledge to faith, the value of learning, or the great services of science to revelation. All that is as public as the daylight, and has gone into the common places. But you will remember that mental activity never yet, since man lived, made a strong nation, a permanent commonwealth, a pure society, virtuous households, or peace in any soul, or a certainty of a future life, or a prayer. As between right and wrong, good and evil, honor and shame, bare knowledge of itself stands by, a looker-on, neutral and non-committal. It is undirected power. It *constructs* or with equal skill it *picks* the lock, in the great "Safe" of the world's welfare. It drives the train freighted with human lives across the continent, or drives it into the chasm. The first fact we have to face is not that *we are dealing with religion* but that *God is dealing with us*, and He deals with us *directly*, not through the brain only but through the conscience and the heart. He speaks to the spiritual part in us, that part which alone can receive Him, hear Him, answer Him, feel

Him, or know Him. It is common to man. It is quite as apt to be strong and clear in persons without much culture, as in those who are pre-occupied with their accomplishments. Spiritual things are spiritually discerned. No principle in philosophy, or law of nature, is surer than that. Spiritual truth is spiritually found out not by any physical organ or intellectual sharpness or energy. Spiritual light enters by a spiritual eye. Of the twelve men who changed the course of the world, in the time of the Cæsars, only one had a remarkable brain or literary training. The Cæsars and their courts knew nothing of them. It is a common salvation, and whoever has not this kind of faith, a child's faith, has not the faith that saves.

"Lord, I have fasted, I have prayed,
And sackcloth has my girdle been,
To purge my soul I have essayed
With hunger blank and vigil keen.
O God of mercy! why am I
Still haunted by the self I fly?

Sackcloth is a girdle good,
O bind it round thee still;
Fasting, it is angels' food,
And Jesus loved the night air chill;
Yet think not prayer and fasts were given
To make one step 'twixt earth and heaven"

O SAVIOUR of the world, who didst send forth thine apostles to proclaim to mankind Thy common salvation, and who hast ordained the way of salvation to be the way of the baptism of water and the Spirit, deliver us, we beseech Thee, from all errors of the mind and sinfulness of heart, that in Thee only we may find the path of safety and walk steadfastly in it unto the end. We ask it for Thy great name's sake, O Christ, our Lord. *Amen.*

Second Monday.

THE COMPREHENSIVE PRINCIPLE.

"He that is faithful in that which is least is faithful in much." Put to the mind alone, as if that were all there is of us, the mind might ask doubtfully how it can be true. Speaking only of people as you know them, or of their lives as they look, you might say it *seems* otherwise. It looks as if one might be upright in large transactions and yet careless in trifles, tell the truth commonly but not always, represent the thing as it is when great interests are at stake, but color or distort it in order to be entertaining or clever; might serve an employer up to the letter of the contract, but no further; might keep the law of the school under the teacher's eye, but break it out of sight; might be devout at church, but irreverent in speech or manners in mixed companies; and so meet emergencies quite handsomely in business, or the family, or religion, and yet in the commonplaces of every-day affairs come short. We have seen such lives. Perhaps you are inclined to excuse some such shortcomings in yourself. What, then, can the saying mean? Christ says that faithful men and faithful women are faithful everywhere, under all conditions, in all places alike.

"Faithful," full of faith. The Master chooses that word. It is the key to the sentence. He does *not* say of any men that they are at all times equally careful or punctual or scrupulous or amiable, or even devout. He names a quality that is deeper, and more comprehensive. Faithfulness is not a single virtue, or a separate trait. Where it is found at all it runs through the whole character, as blood does through the body. The root of it is faith in God, and itself is the root of all excellencies and all moralities. Place the faithful man where you please, try him as you will, he is the same man. Faithfulness is not a thing of more or less, of seasons or opportunities, of rich or poor, of self-interest or respectability, of ornament or convenience. Principles never are, and faithfulness is a principle. It is not to be measured or weighed, nor is it bought or sold, in any market, at any price. You cannot dilute it, or halve it, or cut it into fractions. It is, or else it is not. Whoever has it goes up among the high and strong souls, walks through the world trusted, tells the truth whatever it costs, is chaste and temperate in the light and in the dark, never *fails* whatever he may *lose*, always succeeds with the only real success, sits in heavenly places on the earth, though they may be hard or painful places; and he will live and reign forever with Christ.

Moralists have always been trying to find an absolute foundation for the rules and obligations of a good life, like self-interest, innate sentiment, a social compact, the greatest good of the greatest number. Christ places that foundation beyond all circumstances, all the shifting moods or conditions of the races, and nations, and governments, and ages of men; He plants it in the will of God, manifest in His own life and love. Duty is universal because God is universal. Duty is unchangeable because God is unchangeable. Duty is in the smallest things because God is there. There is no moral system in history like this—man's life having its law, its sanctity, its light, its power, where it has its source, in its Father. Out of this one Fountain came the two united and inseparable strengths and glories of the Gospel, the loving Fatherhood of God and the loving brotherhood of men, each seen equally bright and perfect in Him who is the Son of God and Son of Man; out of this comes the double commandment of the Lord's new law; out of this the doctrines of the creeds; out of this the heavenly and earthly calling of every Christian man and woman; and out of this, finally, the ceaseless business of the Church, the building of holy character Godward and manward, in faith and charity. Hence, too, it is that it is the morality of Christ and the Church alone which sheds splendor and dignity on the little things and common things of life, lifting the least and lowest of them up, and setting them by the side of the greatest. It was in the song of the virgin mother before her Son was born: "He hath exalted them of low degree"—things as well as persons. Christianity, of all the religions of the world, is the religion of common people, common places, common things.

To be sure, this idea has gone more or less into the imagination and the literature of our later times. But it has gone there because it was first in Jesus of Nazareth. You will not find it in the stories and epics, the courts and games, the legends and fables before Mary brought forth her Son and laid Him in a manger. Even now, when genius sets itself to magnify the importance of small things, it is mostly in the fancy of poets. The object is not so much to make us see the real value that the least duties have in themselves to character and to God's judgment, as to show how they lead on, by striking and singular links, to larger things; how

> "We stride the river daily at its spring,
> Nor in our childish thoughtlessness foresee
> What myriad vassal-streams shall tribute bring,
> How like an equal it shall greet the sea."

One writer, himself an artist, tells you, in a fascinating mixture of biography and fiction, of the painter who ransacked old chronicles and travelled through many lands to find a subject for his pencil, and finally came upon it in a group of peasants at his own door, sketching their figures with chalk on the head of a barrel, for a picture that became immortal. Another, the prose-poet of modern England, points out how the finger of the Creator works as marvellously "in the casting of a lump of clay by the roadside as in the kindling of the day-star, or in the lifting of the mountains which are the pillars of heaven." You read entertaining anecdotes of slight causes determining momentous issues, a chance word spoken, a shower interrupting a journey, an accident in a nursery, or a freak of the wind, turning finally the destinies of kingdoms, or colonies, or armies, or great men's reputations. There are books full of such curiosities. They have their use.

But there is something much deeper, more searching and personal and religiously practical to ourselves than that. These "least things," in which each of us is faithful or faithless, are not only the beginnings of what seems great in the eyes of men; they are great already, by what they come out of; they are disclosures of a life within us; they signify a principle in the springs and workings of character; they uncover and they *prove* that inward frame and habit of the soul on which eternal life depends.

"My every weak, though good, design
  O'errule or change as seemeth meet.
Jesus, let all my work be thine!
  Thy work, O Lord, is all complete
And pleasing in Thy Father's sight,
Thou only hast done all things right.

Here then to Thee Thine own I leave;
  Mould as Thou wilt Thy passive clay:
But let me all Thy stamp receive
  But let me all Thy words obey
Serve with a single heart and eye,
And to Thy glory live and die!"

O THOU who hast instructed us in Thy holy Word that Thou wilt accept no divided service, cover us with the helmet of hope and the shield of Thy glorious defence against every temptation; that, being clad in the whole armor of God, and helped by Thee in all time of our necessity, we may enter into the joy of them that love Thee with the whole heart; through Jesus Christ our Lord. *Amen.*

Second Tuesday.

TWO ILLUSIONS.

I THINK we indulge and excuse ourselves in what we call small faults by an unconscious habit of dividing up our inward man into parts, calling them faculties or propensities, and then going on to put off the blame upon them as if they were real and responsible agents apart from ourselves. I hear people say, "Pride embittered me; fear betrayed me into falsehood; anger unsettled my reason; a love of admiration stained my modesty; a love of money drew me on to gambling speculations; love beguiled me; appetite corrupted me." What then are pride and fear and anger and vanity and avarice and lust? Moods, propensities, passions, you say. But whose moods, whose propensities, whose passions but your own? At the centre of them all, the ruler and royal master of them all, stands your will, having ears to hear the voice of God. That will-power makes you what you are, marks and bounds your personality, parts you off from all the souls about you, drags you out from under all screens and shadows into daylight; having reason and conscience and Bible and Church to help you if you will take their warning and their grace. While your inclinations were having riot, where were you? Manhood or womanhood is not a medley of brute forces, or a menagerie of wild impulses, or a mob of lawless passions. By that will-power you are either saving or wasting your life. By that will-power, set wrong or set right, you are every day rising to the righteousness of Christ, or sinking to spiritual death. By the will-power in you you are climbing towards a sure Heaven, or drifting out on a dark sea. Looking down upon you, and into the secrets of your soul, God loves you too well to let you be deceived. It is you that He calls His child by your name; you that He cares for; you that He watches, pities, helps; and it is with you that He will reckon for that which is "least." Behind every wrong act, every neglected duty,—the hasty word, the impatient gesture, the equivocating answer, the jealous cruelty, the reckless calumny, is yourself. Each came out of your whole character; not your temperament, or your constitution, or your provocation, but yourself. You say it was unconsidered;

but it was you that did not consider. You say you did not think; but God made you a thinking creature, and your thinking faculty was not given you for great occasions, which are rare in any life, and are not what will fix your place when you give in your account. Trace the secret history of any of the great crimes which now so often disgrace the business world, and you find that he who is unjust in much was unjust first in that which is least. "A good tree cannot bring forth evil fruit."* Out of the one heart are the issues of life and death. Another illusion that misleads us is a habit of estimating actions by their outward or apparent effects; not by their absolute and essential quality as being good or bad in themselves; not by comparing them with a fixed and eternal standard, which is the law of God; not by their secret but sure effect on our own spiritual salvation. It is a difficulty that runs all through our ceaseless warfare, between the world outside and the law within, between flesh and spirit, between self and Christ. What we see and hear, touch, work in, eat

* Our Lord pictures it in two perfect figures: "Make the tree good, and the fruit will be good." "The light of the body is the eye. If thine eye be single, thy whole body shall be full of light."

and wear, lay up and display, is so conspicuous and ever-present that we make it a measure even of what is infinitely greater than all of it—ourselves. We take what is external to us, coarse and perishing matter at the best, and apply its fluctuating valuations to the part of us which opens into the world above us, which receives gifts from God, is a child of God, and grows, if it will, into the measure of the stature of the man perfect in Christ. In business-dealing with a customer, a contractor or client, a partner or a clerk, I take some advantage, seen by me, not seen by him, giving me a trifling credit, which, if he did see it, he would say belonged not to me but to him. By the material or visible account it is small. The transaction looks not exactly like a theft, but it looks not at all like honor. Shall I go back and set the wrong right? or do I say to myself, "It is too trifling a matter; let it go." Then the everlasting law of commercial faithfulness is broken, and I am a thief.

A woman at the head of a house, who imagines herself a Christian, lets a servant or seamstress or milliner go unpaid from month to month, denying herself no comfort, feeling scarcely a twinge of conscience, and calls it a trivial neglect. But there is a sentence in God's law which declares that precise trifle to have a judgment-cry in it which reaches the ears of the Lord of Hosts. By an unchaste word, or gesture, or fashion, you leave a spot on some man's or woman's imagination which all the repentances of a life-time will not wash out. You will not whiten the stain, or make it little, by an adjective. You are at school, and you go on committing and hiding petty disobediences. Every one of them leaves the school-law broken, and it leaves the crystal of your soul's purity cracked. You know what you would say to the dealer at the shop who apologized for the flaw in the jewel he sold you, that it was a little flaw. Who has put into your mortal mind balances by which you dare to pronounce that one ugly deed of yours is big and another is insignificant, in the ever-winding and far-reaching issues of eternity? Not He certainly who tells you what heavenly rewards there are for a cup of cold water, and what fearful penalties hang on a word spoken against the Holy Ghost,—tells you that to take into your arms a poor woman's child, to rest and bless the mother, is better for you than to clasp diamond bracelets upon them; tells you that to serve your brother even to the washing of his feet is more royal than the robing of a queen or the crowning of a king.

Here, at least, in this serious time, you long to be more like Him whose purity you worship, whose name you speak with every prayer, whose cross is on your foreheads, whose love, you know, is greater and sweeter than the dearest human love in your hearts. Confess, then, that it is these faults, half-open and half-hidden, which separate you from Him. Faults, do you say? Be honest and call them *sins*. Your conscience is not dead. You believe the Creed. You venerate and perhaps love your Church. You say your prayers. You hope you will not be lost out of the Family when your Father gathers His children to Him at the end. Yet you know that all these holy realities are far above the level of your daily temper and behavior. When you lift your eyes towards them, they seem out of your reach. They scarcely touch your poor, unworthy, sinful life. *Here* you see so much that is weak, yielding, unsteadfast, vain, mean, wicked; *there* the clear tranquillity and glory of the Father's House on high. How can you bring that better and nobler life and this poor, daily struggle together, make them one, and live that one life with Christian joy and power?

Two ways have been tried. One is to begin on the outside, watch the faults, study them, analyze them, name them, make a catalogue of them, and set up before you a list of religious rules against them You deal with them in detail, one by one. You station your sentinels in the morning, and call them in and take their reports at night. These are the rules, and here are the shortcomings. You try and try again. This is the way of the law. It has its place, and its use. We are so made that written regulations yield a certain amount of help. Some people are more helped by them than others. In the progress of every individual disciple, as in the public history of the world, there comes in what may be called the law-period, when the statute is put before the eyes, and the passions that would sweep us to perdition are "held in by bit and bridle," the threat of a just punishment checks us, forbidden things are fought back in that fear,—"Thou shalt" and "Thou shalt not" sounding in our ears. Israel was governed by rule, and you and I have an Israel, a Moses, and stone-tablets in our breast. Christ did not come to destroy this law power, by His Gospel, but to fulfil it, or fill it full. I have known scrupulous persons who were largely indebted to this legal regimen, and there was the strength of granite pillars in their characters. But there is a limit to that stern statute on the stone, and to the help it gives. There are wells of living water, there are fountains of healing faith, there are streams of the heart's best blood of love, which rules alone will not open. There are great springs of spiritual power in the soul,—penitence, prayer, charity,—which are never reached by a rod, or stirred by penalties. Something more is wanted. What then is the other way? It is the way Christ took and taught. He sets the heart right first,—the inner man. The beginning of all goodness in us, He says, is to get this heart close to Him, conscious of Him, quickened by Him, communing in a sacrament with Him, alive with His life. You will love what He loves, hate what He hates, go where He calls, let alone whatever separates you from Him. One place will be like another to your conscience because He is there. One word spoken or deed done—right or wrong—will be like another, because it is either for or against His will. The thought of Him will be law enough. As there can be no strong morality without religion, so there will be no consistent and steady righteousness in you except by this living and loving faith towards a living and loving Lord.

Your baptism is to pledge you this free spirit of adoption as a son or a daughter of God. Your confirmation is to pour out upon you more and more this spirit of an adopted and consecrated child, which is liberty and joy. Your Communion-Feast is to nourish in you this high, and sweet, and growing life. Christian character will be one thing. Each duty will be a privilege; you will go to it not as a slave scourged to the plantation, but as a free man, liberated from your lameness, walking, leaping, and praising God. Selfishness will be a mortification to you. Sin will be shame, the fore-fire of hell. Self-sacrifice will be a victory. This more and more, till nothing, great or small, easy or hard, no height or depth, not things present or things to come, not the principalities of the world, or the frivolities of fashion, or any other creature shall be able to separate you from the love of God which is in Christ Jesus, your Lord. "The whole body is full of light."

Saints are made saints not by doing extraordinary or uncommon things, but by doing common things in an uncommon way, on uncommonly high principles, [illegible] an uncommonly self-sacrificing spirit. Be sure [illegible] the only substantial thing. The bits of [illegible] hat we call our learning, the bits of property that we call our wealth, the momentary vanities of delight that we call the conquests of social life,—how swiftly they hurry to their graves, or are lost in forgetfulness! Nothing, nothing else but character survives, and character is Christ formed within. The proof of the true man,—where is it found? Not in the size of his performances, but in the fibre of his manhood; not in the quantity, or occasions, or noise of his actions, but in the uprightness of his soul. You will not have to wait to see how large the trusts are which are committed to his keeping, or how he will behave himself in some signal emergency. The world is a safer and stronger place on account of him, and Heaven is more real. "I will show you to whom he is like. He is like a man which built a house, and digged deep, and laid the foundation on a rock."

"Whate'er thou lovest best,
E'en that become thou must.
Christ's, if thou lovest Christ,
Dust, if thou lovest dust."

O GOD, the Perfect Truth and Everlasting Light, who hast made faith in Thy Son to be the beginning of man's salvation and the foundation of all righteousness: Enlighten and strengthen our hearts by Thy Spirit, that, believing Thy word, and confessing that which we believe, we may be made like unto Thy Son Christ in His everlasting kingdom and glory through the same Christ Our Lord. *Amen.*

Third Wednesday.

CREED AND CONDUCT.

SLOWLY, very slowly does the Church learn and put into her life her Lord's constant lesson—simple and clear as it is—that His religion is neither a creed without conduct, nor conduct without a creed. The Church's weakness is our weakness; her fault is our fault. We put asunder what God has joined together. We take a part rather than the whole, and get half the blessing. Why is it? Is it not evidently because we allow in ourselves one or another one-sidedness? If the temperament is inactive, and the will weak, a kind of speculative indolence in us says, "Religion is a thing to be *believed;* the doctrine of works is a snare; 'doing' is a vain delusion, it is even 'deadly'; this is a bad world enough, to be sure, but God will take care of it; let me only be orthodox and safe; Heaven forbid that I should do anything that would look as if I expected to be saved by my performances." If, on the other hand, the temperament is lively and the will energetic, if the executive faculty is uppermost and the view is practical, and the spiritual sensibilities are dull, then the bustling force in us says, "Religion is something to be *done;* no matter about your dogmas and articles of faith; the world wants reforming, society is wrong and needs to be set right, and nothing will do that but labor; let me busy myself not about a world overhead, or a world to come, but the world that is at hand and palpable; here are business and philanthropies, I will find my salvation in them."

One way of disposing of these halfnesses is to let them alone, concluding comfortably that one will balance the other, and that between the mystics on one side and the workers on the other mankind will get on, we ourselves drifting on whichever tide happens to suit our inclination. This was not the way or the teaching of our Master, or of the apostolic men whom He filled with His Spirit, and illuminated with His truth. The first good and the first greatness of the world is personal character, not a scheme of theological opinions, or a scheme of social reformation. Character is an integral and not a fragmentary thing. It is a symmetrical growth, having laws, proportions and vital conditions of its own. It cannot be a practical force without having its root in unseen realities, and its conscious source in the living God, and its perpetually replenished supply by communion with Him. It cannot be a developed and healthy saint without a constant putting forth of its vitality and vigor in a principled activity of use and exercises of righteousness.

The Master came not only to tell us to live rightly, and to show us how to live rightly, but to create in us the power to live rightly. Here is the difference between all false religions and the one that alone is true. No other teacher, no other leader, no other prophet, priest or king has done that. Faith is the laying hold of that power. The very statement shows the twofold nature of Christianity. If it were action, and nothing but action, there would be no laying hold, no reaching up, no drinking in, no prayer, no praise, no sacramental refreshment, no receiving of gifts; the sky would be an impenetrable ceiling stretched over our heads. If it were faith, and nothing but faith, then why speak of it as a power at all? An unexpended power, an unused force, a fountain with no stream, a fruit-tree with no fruit—these are names and images not of life, but of death. "Faith without works is dead."

A saying of Mr. Matthew Arnold has become familiar by quotation, to the effect that "conduct is four-fifths of life," the inference being that a Christian man's doings are four times as important as his believing. Mr. Arnold was a better critic than philosopher. He often said things so well that they were taken to be true because they were well said. One cannot help wondering how he made his measurements when he propounded this definite statement of the relative dimensions of faith and work. He must have known that everything done on earth that is worth doing is believed in before it is done; *i. e.*, that before, behind, beneath, above all effectual or memorable action, in enterprise, in invention, in education, in building, or colonizing or conquering, no less than in the Church, there must be a creed. You have four-fifths of a watch without the mainspring, four-fifths of a steamer without the engine, four-fifths of a man without his heart and brain. It was a witty enough answer of Clarkson, the philanthropist, to the canting pietist, who inquired of him the state of his soul, that he was so busy with his work that he had no time to think whether he had a soul. But without his soul he never would have found his work. It is a bad fashion, bad logic, and bad manners to glorify modern Christendom and deny the eternal Christ.

On the other hand, the world has a right to look worshippers, as they come out of church, in the face, and ask them, What do you bring away from your altar, your psalm, your sermon, your benediction? What gifts have you to distribute in your neighborhood? Why should we go in and say your Creed with you? Whatever else the world knows, it knows that it wants good, hearty, honest, cheerful, righteous work. It is a very unfinished world. As you look in among its frightful and needless inequalities, its mean competitions, its tyrannies, falsehoods, insincerities, superstitions, disorders, bad temper, bad air, bad faith, turn to the Master who has come from Heaven to change, to renew, to heal, to toil, to suffer, to save, and say to Him, "Hear am I; take me; guide me; without Thee nothing is strong, nothing is holy; work Thou within me, and let me work and live with Thee!"

"Whether there many be who thrive
In their vast suit for that vast love,
Truly I know not; this I know,
That love lives not in outward show,

That but to seek is not to strive,
That thankless praises, empty prayers,
Can claim no bond, for will of theirs
His court to move.

"Whether there many be or few
Elect, the heavenly goal to win,
Truly I know not; this I know
That none who move with footsteps slow,
That none who fight with hearts untrue,
That none who serve with service cold,
The eternal city can behold,
Or enter in."

WORK Thy work in us, O Lord, that, believing in Thee and in Thy Word with a contrite and true heart, we may ever obey Thee, not in servile fear, but with cheerful, readiness and a consistent righteousness, and thus through the path of obedience come to dwell and reign with Thee, who, being obedient to the Father even unto death, livest and reignest with Him and the Holy Spirit, world without end. *Amen.*

Third Thursday.

VOICES WITHIN.

When the Spirit speaks to us from day to day, or in some rare moment of searching tenderness, and tells us that, hard as our hearts may be, and poor as our present way of living is with its frivolous pleasures and mean pursuits and its indifference to the high things of faith, nevertheless there is actually somewhere in us, not utterly dead, a desire for better satisfactions, do we disbelieve that? Does one of you reply, "I know nothing about this divine thirst; Bible men, psalmists and penitents and pulpits may say what they please; I am content as I am"?

Look farther and closer. Take first that part of your time which you spend in work, does the occupation satisfy you without God? Clearly enough we were made to be working creatures. It is stamped into us, through and through, that labor of one kind or another, of hands or brain, is the law of the whole living creation. At the very head of the universe stands a working God. "My Father worketh hitherto, and I work." What a comfort that text is for men and for women who feel overburdened with toil! We wish there were less to be done, but if we stop doing, most of us pretty soon become restless rather than resting, acting in mischievous directions, or else we find forces of unhappiness coming into action because the better powers are disused. You think the birds in the branches have an easy time, but watch one for a few hours, and you find that bird-life is about as anxious, vigilant and laborious as your own. The animal world, the intellectual, the moral, the spiritual world live by work. Even the unconscious atoms of nature, from the stars to the vegetable atoms, toil incessantly. If we will not live to work, we are obliged to work to live. The spiritual world is a working reality, as much as the farm or shop. Acknowledge it or not, you are a spiritual creature, and unless you take your spiritual wants to Christ to be healed and guided and sanctified by Him, you are but a mutilated fragment and failure of a man. And something about your outward work tells you this. Sometimes you are perplexed about it, feeling the need of more wisdom and more patience in it than you can give yourself. That is really a thirst after God, whose wisdom and patience alone are infinite, and from whom alone these strong gifts can come. At other times you feel your task to be greater than your capacity. You sorely want more power than you have and are half discouraged. That want is a thirst for God, because He alone can supply the power, or else can encourage you to persevere without it. Sometimes there comes a better feeling yet. In some hour of more than ordinary sobriety you will be thinking over your whole course of works and living and you will ask, what all this daily labor is for, what is the object and what the end. Is it merely to keep body and soul together, to get wages and eat them up, or to set up a little better furniture than your neighbors, is that all, or are the enlargement of your soul, charity to your neighbors, the glory of conquering self, the eternal life gained, the salvation of yourself and others,—are these the real end? This too is thirsting after God, the living God, who would not leave you easy or let you be truly strong till you come for strength to Him.

From your outward occupations suppose you turn inward to the life within yourself. First there is a mind there. Being a part of yourself it has always gone along with you; you have never stopped to study it much. Not professing to be a philosopher, you have attempted no explanation of its constitution or classification of its qualities. But there it is, the part of you that thinks, observes, learns, reasons, and remembers. More than all this, it looks forward, and it looks up. You may have let it alone, but it would not let you alone. There are moments when your thought would run away from all the present scene. Call it back, or turn it off, or choke it down, or befool it with trifles, as you would, it kept telling you of a world not seen by your eyes, and a life not yet begun. Where is that world? Am I ever going to it? What will it be like? When that other life begins, whereabouts will it find me? If I live on now wholly for things that are going to perish,—when they are gone what shall I shall have left? Must not He who made me always have power over me? And if so, how will it be if I am against Him? Can I be safe, or saved, unless He and I are friends? These are the questions. Some such words as these will be breaking from honest lips, "My mind crieth out for the living God." "He only can make it well with me, safe to live, safe to die. Without Him it will be all death, and worse than death."

Along with this intellectual part of you speaks another part, your conscience. Look where you will, either into the interior world of thought, or around you, you see that some things are right, others wrong. There is one indelible, unalterable, everlasting division line. Unprincipled men have been trying—by their politics and their sophistries—for six thousand years, to blur over or blot out that distinction, to make right things look wrong, or wrong things as good as right, trying to get out of the way the troublesome difference between "Thou shalt," and "Thou shalt not."

They have never bridged the gulf, or lessened it by the thousandth part of the breadth of a hair. They have only broken their own bones and gone down. So at every step there is a warfare; selfishness, passion, sin, fighting, all the way, from cradle to grave, against love, purity, holiness. Very often the battle goes hard. Worse yet, it goes wrong, and then there is misery. Self-accusation and shame swell in the breast; retributions of inward agony; other people made wretched,—these and other penalties are what make the earth so unlike heaven, and keep the whole creation groaning and travailing in pain together until now. We must be made of quite different stuff from what we are to escape these baptisms of fire. Name them as you please, their only remedy is in a suffering and forgiving Lord, honoring the law, but healing the law-breaker by a saving sacrifice. And therefore the meaning of their cry is, "I am athirst for God," "like a dry and thirsty land where there is no water." David wrote that in a wilderness, and a wilderness is where you feel yourself to be.

Mind and conscience are not all. We are made for love. Affections tie us together in families, and in larger circles. By their wondrous attractions the life of others becomes a part of ourselves, and from that moment the joy of living, in many cases all that makes life worth having at all, depends on being loved by them. What boundless possibilities of suffering enter by that door! Suffering from not being loved enough, from being loved too much, from being forgotten, from injury and ingratitude, from all the variety of ills befalling those that are dearest, by the separations of distance, by disease, by death, by sin. Strike these all out and you would go far to transfigure the vale of misery itself into a Paradise. God is love. He alone loves enough and not too much, never forgets, never changes, never disappoints, never fails, never slumbers, never dies. In Christ He takes the sympathies and affections of man; His love becomes a human love, yet wiser than any man's, in tenderness passing the love of woman, all-patient, all-enduring. Can we frame the faintest conception of an affection like that without desiring the mercy of it? It has been disputed whether there are really any such things as broken hearts. There certainly are enough that are terribly bruised; and there is not a habitation on earth where some heart does not want a love that the world cannot give.

Turn the cry of nature into the supplication of faith. Let the unconscious need of God pass into the free confession of the new man, His penitent child. Go home to your Father. Sit down at the table with the Son. "Let him that is athirst come."

> "'Tis mercy all that Thou hast brought
> My mind to seek her peace in Thee;
> Yet while I seek but find Thee not,
> No peace my wandering soul shall see.
> Is there a thing beneath the sun
> That strives with Thee my heart to share?
> Ah, tear it thence, and reign alone,
> The Lord of every motion there!"

O THOU, Almighty Father, who hast created and formed us, who hast put into our minds desires which this world cannot fill, and longings which nothing on the earth can satisfy, draw us, we beseech Thee, unto Thyself and replenish our souls with heavenly light and strength out of thine infinite abundance. Help us in every place to see Thee, in every weakness to lean upon Thee, in every temptation to flee to Thee for deliverance, and in all our work to seek Thy favor, which is our life. Scatter our doubts and relieve all our necessities; and to that end, dispose us to the faith which overcomes the world, through Christ our Lord. *Amen.*

Third Friday.

DIVINE LOVE AND FIRE.

"GOD is love," and "Our God is a consuming fire." We all want to know about God,—what kind of a God He is, why He made us, how He feels towards us, what He will do with us. Without having these questions start and stirred in him no one would go to church, or pray, or even live and *think*, many years. They open the whole secret of religion.

St. John says, "God is love." He speaks from knowledge and on authority. He is a disciple specially loved, of a loving nature, thoroughly instructed, inspired by the Holy Spirit. He also says, "He that loveth not knoweth not God," and that is profoundly true. Only love can know what love is. Only friends can know what friendship is.

Another disciple, whose words are in the same Book, on the same authority, taught by the same Master, inspired by the same Spirit, says, "God is a consuming fire." They are both speaking of the same God,—the Father of our Lord Jesus Christ,—our God and our Father. At first, on the surface of it, and to most people, it seems like a flat contradiction. Yet both are in God's Word, and as Christians we know that God cannot contradict Himself.

We shall, perhaps, get the best clue to the difficulty by going back to the Garden of Eden. What took place there is the key to the whole mystery. The story of the first man and woman is the story of the human race, of each human heart.

"Adam and his wife hid themselves from the presence of the Lord God among the trees of the garden." We are not apt to hide ourselves from those who love us, unless their love is ill-judged or obtrusive or merely sentimental. One would suppose this man and woman had reason enough to believe what St. John wrote four thousand years afterwards was true, that God is love. He had made them both, and given them to each other, and so far neither of them had known disappointment, failure, old age, bodily pain or heart-ache. The garden itself, they knew, was of God's forming and planting and blossoming, not an unsightly spot, a blasted tree, a drought, or blight, or mildew, or frost, or breath of malarial air in it. Even in our

June or October the face of the earth, with all its beauty and sweetness, is less perfect than the primitive Paradise was. Every faculty in them for healthy work and worship they knew to be God's gift, and they were living in a universe of light and freedom, set in order for them by His Hand. That morning they had worshipped Him with thanksgiving. Why should they now, as the sun sets, hide themselves at His voice, and why should Adam answer, "I was afraid"?

Something has happened, and that something has changed the relations, the feelings, the intercourse, not only between the man and the woman, but between man and his God. God is not to the man what He was before. Before, God was love; now He is a consuming fire. When he went out that day to his business of trailing the vines and dressing the ground,—"No more toil," as poetry says, "of the sweet gardening labor than sufficed for wholesome rest and appetite,"—he would have been *glad* to hear the heavenly voice, or to see his Father's face anywhere; now he cowers and skulks behind the trees. Whose fault is it? Has God changed towards man or has man changed towards God? That question is of tremendous import to us, every one. It strikes into the inmost heart of our faith. It goes to the bottom of belief and unbelief. It cuts up a thousand excuses, doubts, discontents, by the roots, and scatters delusions from our minds. The right answer to it would settle a controversy which has been going on ever since Adam's day, and which has filled great libraries with elaborate books. Notice that God's answer to it was twofold; one answer was a hand of loving-kindness still stretched out unchanged to man, to every man, from generation to generation, to this day, with a Father's protection and pity, *because "God is love";* the other answer was a flaming sword set up over the gate of the way that leads to the Tree of life, because "God is a consuming fire." This dreary effort to hide from God, going on among the sons and daughters of men, always has been the most hopeless and unprofitable of all human undertakings. Yet have you never tried to do it, or wished you could do it, yourself—either from an accusing conscience, or because you thought of God as a stranger, altogether unlike yourself, in whose presence you were uneasy?

Before we begin to complain of the law of retribution, we are to see how we got where we are. Adam had broken a commandment, and "the old Adam" that does that is in us. The old Adam may have been getting gradually dead and buried in us since we were born again, but he comes to life in us every day. God says to us, "This fruit, My child, will hurt you; this pleasant-tasting poison, this lovely-looking indulgence, this wrong thing, this sin of any kind, it was not meant for you; let it alone. I know; I made *you*, and I made the fruit. I forbid you to taste it because sooner or later and in one way or another it will make you miserable. I do not want you to be miserable." "God is love." If you abuse your body by intemperance, by gluttony, by sensuality of any sort, by unhealthy habits, your body will be hurt by some one of those various kinds of torture which are stationed in all parts of it, like alarm-bells on the road to danger, to save you, if you will have sense enough to be saved. If you allow anger or envy or spite in yourself, it will eat into your soul, and eat out your peace of mind or your respect among your neighbors. If you cheat or lie, either the courts or your conscience will chastise you. If you sin in any way, in the light or in the dark, in a passion or in cool blood, your sin will find you out. You will try to hide, but you cannot hide. You have been eating of the tree of the knowledge of evil; and you will hear the voice of the Lord God calling your name,—perhaps the same night, perhaps long afterwards, perhaps after you have slept in a grave and waked up at the judgment; you will hear Him, and fear will strike all through and through your soul. Then will come what Christ makes a picture of to warn you in His parable of Dives and the beggar,—the separation, the gulf fixed, the cry out of torment for a drop of water, the "fire" within you, and on your tongue. God has not changed. He is the same God of love that He was when He made you, and fitted you for virtue and honor, and made the world beautiful like Eden for you to live in. He cannot shift as you shift, go where you go, be unclean as you are unclean, break up His divine plan, unhinge His blessed order, "deny Himself" because you "deny Him." You have done what you could to change Him, to baffle Him, to get around Him, to drag Him down; and your failure to break the Rock and ruin the universe has broken your bones. Satan told you—you women and you men—as he told your mother, "You shall not surely die; sin is sweet, take it." You believed the lie and took it. You have turned what was the tenderest and truest "love" into a "consuming fire." Who is to blame?

"Forgive me that I, looking for the day,
Forget whence it must shine,
And turn Thy helps to reasons for delay,
And love not Thee, but Thine.
And I have knelt, how often, thanking Thee
For gifts Thy love hath given,
Then turned away to bend to these my knee,
And seek in these my Heaven.

"On me, unworthy, shed, O Lord, the glow
Of Thy dear light and love,
That I may walk with trusting faith below
Towards the fair land above.
That I may learn in Thy sharp strokes to see
The love that on me smiled,
And find in all I have a thought of Thee,
Who still hast blessed Thy child!"

O LORD JESUS, the patient Healer of our souls, create in us by the merciful fire of Thy chastisements a pure heart and a right spirit. Repair that heavenly image which is defaced in us by sin; pour into our penitent hearts the oil of gladness, and adorn our deformity with the beauty of Thy righteousness, O Christ; that being restored by Thy compassion we may worship and serve Thee acceptably, with the Father and the Holy Ghost, world without end. *Amen.*

Third Saturday.

WHAT THE FIRE CONSUMES.

WE have been taught that love may be a fire. Now let us see what it is that the fire consumes. As love has two qualities, making the heart where it lives larger and sweeter, and at the same time blessing the other life where it is received, so fire has two. I speak of it as it is in nature, not as we see it burning uncontrolled in the weak or careless hands of men; it consumes, and it purifies. It sweeps across a marsh or swamp, in autumn, a field covered with a mass of rank, decaying and unhealthy grass and weeds, and leaves it cleansed; it catches in a tangled thicket a nest of unclean vermin, and presently a heap of pure ashes prepares the soil for nutritious husbandry; it rages through the dry branches of an old forest, and there rises on the spot a harvest of grain or a growth of better timber; it eats into a pestilential bog, and burns away death for life. If these inaninate things that are burnt had sensibility, as our flesh and nerves have, they would smart and scream under this purifying process. Life and health are precious, and so they are costly, in the body and the soul. They are worth what they cost. Birth, conversion, repentance, redemption, are all painful. Old Testament and New Testament show us that, and our every-day experience shows it just as plainly. You cannot conquer your faults and get them under your feet without a battle with yourself as full of distress as any fought with sword or shot. You have found it harder, perhaps, to be generous to a rival whom you dislike, to pray for one who has slandered you, to "turn away wrath" with "a soft answer," to confess a fault, to govern your tongue, to be reverent and pure in a company where there is profanity or indecency, than to draw blood from your arm or to hold your finger in a flame. "Our God is a consuming fire." These laws of life and death, of sin and recovery, of a struggle with temptation and a new heart, are His ways of working—working in you and working out your salvation. Do they not make it plainer how the same God is "Love," and a "consuming fire"? *You* are not consumed. Your worst enemy within you is consumed. The garden of the world is not burnt up;

if its iniquities, its wrongs, its cruelties, its uncleannesses, its plague spots, its dishonestics are, let us be thankful. If these horrible evils last, then the fire must last, and be "everlasting fire," because God is eternally good, not because He is eternally angry. He did not burn up Eden; He drove the man and his wife out of it. They drove themselves out by their disobedience; and that was their "fire." So it was with Dives; so it is with rich men and poor men, too, to-day, who will not let themselves be purged of their selfishness, and will not be "persuaded, though one rose from the dead;" so with Ahab and Jezebel, Ananias and Sapphira, Judas, Herod, some Pharisees, many unrepenting sinners in every rank of society who "have ears" and will not "hear." With their own hands they go on preparing the wood and the sulphur, and they kindle the fire.

It is just after the magnificent description, in the twelfth to the Hebrews, where the giving of the law for us at Sinai is seen under the terrific imagery of the mount that burned with a blaze in surrounding "blackness, and darkness, and tempest, and the sound of a trumpet," that we have the text about the consuming fire. One suggests the other. The meaning is that men are in so much danger of going wrong that they need a tremendous power of alarm and pain to keep them right. Law is their first lesson. That sounds into their ears and their consciences; they learn that law leads up to grace—Moses to Christ. The black tempest clears the air for the sunlight on the hills of Eternal Peace; and the fire that consumes becomes the spirit of Life.

When your heart feels one motion in it towards the new life of penitence, faith and prayer, remember that your God is love, your home is your Father's house. When you have sinned, and see your guilt, remember there are no shadows or screens on earth where you can hide from God. Rather go to Him. When you are tempted to harm any man or woman, think of Christ's parable to those who in this life care only for this life's good things. And when you are hindered or discouraged in the way of duty, lift up your eyes to the city of the living God, where are "the Mediator of the new covenant," and "the innumerable company of angels," and "the spirits of the just."

"Beneath Thine hammer, Lord, I lie,
With contrite spirit prone;
O mold me till to self I die,
And live to Thee alone!

With frequent disappointments sore,
  And many a bitter pain,
Thou laborest at my being's core
  Till I be formed again.

"Smite, Lord! Thine hammer's needful wound
  My baffled hopes confess.
Thine anvil is the sense profound
  Of mine own nothingness.
Smite, till, from all its idols free,
  And filled with love divine,
My heart shall know no good but Thee,
  And have no will but Thine!"

O GOD, who art of purer eyes than to behold iniquity, mercifully grant unto us such a sense of uncleanness that we may seek Thy cleansing; such a knowledge and confession of sin that by the fire of Thy love our hearts may be purified; and such amendment of life that we may behold Thee in the brightness of Thy heavenly glory, through Jesus Christ our Lord. *Amen.*

Third Monday.

NO COMPROMISE.

UNEASY at our Lord's piercing rebukes for its faithlessness, its frivolity and its danger, the worldly mind casts about for some relief under the rebuke, some escape from the danger. May it not be that the fierce antagonism in which "the Prince of this world" arrays himself against the Son of Man was something peculiar to His personality, a solitary occurrence, happening once in history, but of no serious concern to other people or other times, at most incidental to a temporary condition of society in the Roman Empire and its licentious Eastern provinces?

But the more steadily we look at His language, the more undeniably it appears that Christ makes Himself there at one with His disciples. He is laying down a law for every Christian life lived there or here, in His time and in our time, in Judæa, and in America. What is true of the Head is just as true of the whole body, and of every member. If selfishness did not overcome, beguile, seduce, or secularize Him, then it will not overcome, or beguile, or seduce, or secularize the Church where the Church is true to Him; where it is filled with His Spirit, and lives His life. And this, not something else, is precisely, and always, and everywhere, the Church's business. The world, on *its* part, we may be sure, has not altered a whit. Its temper, habits and objects, its tyranny, meanness, corruption, falsehood, are now just what they were then,—no matter what changes there have been in the houses it lives in, the clothes that cover it, the language it speaks in, the dishes it cooks, the wines it drinks. Cæsar and Herod and their queens do not make "the world," nor do Rome with its palaces and baths and amphitheatre, or Jerusalem and its slaughter of the Prophets, or Corinth and its sensual games. No! The world makes them, and it makes them over and over again, wherever it can set its foot and work the charm of its sorcery, here, where other flowers and pictures crown the feast; where the temples are Christian and not Pagan; where the traffic is not by caravans, and the robberies are not open on the highways, and the leprosy is not in the flesh. The fashions shift, but fashion is the same thing. The Demas who becomes a bad Christian to-day, who cares more for his social standing than for the Lord who died for him, who goes more eagerly to a frolic, a theatre or a dance than to a Sacrament, who worships the God who made him less heartily than the fortune he has made, and gives fifty times as much to his amusements as to his Saviour—is the same man that forsook St. Paul, and departed to Thessalonica, and died a reprobate, "having loved this present world."

And accordingly, by necessary inference,—these *two* "kingdoms" remaining exactly what they always were, neither of them having changed a particle, the two being in the same radical and fatal opposition to one another which selfishness on the one hand and the love of God and man on the other *must* always be in,—it follows that if now-a-days the Church itself is worldly, if Church men and Church women are very much the same sort of people with the world's people, or if when they come into the Church they bring into it very much the same ways of judging and thinking and feeling, of envying and criticising and slandering and sneering at each other, of getting and wasting and using and abusing money,—in other words, if worldliness itself comes to Church and takes possession of pews and pulpit; if the Church's affairs are managed and its finances are controlled on worldly principles, with worldly ambitions, by worldly men; if the pulpit-message condescends to be only a pious echo of the world's opinion, or a solemn sanction of the world's popularities; if the Fine Arts of the Lord's House, instead of glorifying Christ and His "Beauty of holiness," only minister to the same tastes or indulge the same fancies with the Fine Arts of the Greek chisel, the Corinthian garden, the gallery and the play-house,—then the two kingdoms have somehow got mixed and confounded. Common eyes are puzzled to tell which is which. One side or the other has been betrayed, and there is no need to say which side it is. The Prince of this world has come and has found a great deal in common with him in the body of Christians,—an easy entrance, familiar voices, friendly faces, and a congenial atmosphere.

Can there be any doubt about it? Hear what Christ Himself says to *all* His followers:—"If ye were of the world the world would love his own. But because ye are not of the world, but I have chosen you out of the world, therefore the world hateth you. These, O Father, are not of the world, even as I am not of the world." "If any man love the world, the love of the Father is not in him." In every accent of command, entreaty, warning, by every strenuous remonstrance, this Lord of spiritual life sets the two masters and the two services apart. The Gospel is one long appeal for loyalty to a Heavenly Leader. The apostolic preaching continues it in every variety of expostulation. We can choose the one, or we can choose the other; but we cannot choose both at the same time. The world-spirit in any man poisons, shrivels, kills the soul. Christ's Spirit gives life, longer life, pure life, noble life, victorious life, gives it more abundantly, and makes it life everlasting.

Plainly enough then the work of disenchanting society of its low delusions, of elevating and spiritualizing it, is to begin, as the old prophets did, at the House of God. The first purifying must be in the church itself. Draw the line straight, and cut it deep. You will not cut it too deep. Be reasonable, be large, be patient, be good-natured, but be holy, for God is holy and will be worshipped only in holy ways. Say to worldliness, at the church door, at the altar, at the choir, at the pulpit, "This is holy ground." Remember what the Lord Christ in His indignation did, with the scourge in His hand, in a temple less hallowed than every Christian sanctuary. Let the world come in, by all means, to learn, to listen, to kneel down and confess and pray, to keep Lent, to be converted, baptized and blest; the doors are open wide for that,—but not to desecrate. The Lord is in His holy temple, and all that pertains to its worship and offices is His. Keep it for Him; you will not be sorry when the glitter of life fades, as it will, and its lights go out, and the great realities are revealed before your soul, and the books are opened. If the prince of this world looks in, let him find nothing here of his own.

"How often as we beat along
With wind ahead and flowing strong,
We hear our watchful Captain cry,
'Near! Nothing off!' and 'Full and by!'
So when in life our oars begin
To run the rapids dark of sin,
May conscience wake our timely fear,
Lifting her warning cry of 'Near!'
And when from Truth's unerring line
Our coward lips would dare decline,
Then may we heed, tho' fools should scoff,
Her stern injunction, 'Nothing off!'
Virtue and vice to win us try,
Be then our watchword, 'Full and by!'
Safe course, thro' this world to another,
Is 'full' of one and 'by' the other!"

ALMIGHTY God and most merciful Saviour, while weeks, months, and years are bearing us on toward the time of our appointed change, Thou sittest above the heavens, the same yesterday, to-day, and forever. O Lord, be Thou our strong tower, whereunto we may alway resort. Grant that by faith in Thee our hearts may be fixed, stablished, and settled; that being steadfast in purpose and wise to withstand all the allurements of the prince of this world, we may so pass the waves of this troublesome world, that finally we may come to the land of everlasting life, there to reign with Thee, world without end. *Amen.*

Third Tuesday.

COWARDICE.

An age of active moral impulses is not sure to be an age of moral courage. The religion itself may be social and amiable, intelligent and enterprising, given to missions and philanthropy; but when the spirit of a worldly and fashion-following society sneers or tempts in any of its imposing and fascinating shapes, it is not at all sure that this religion will not do what Simon Peter did at the trial of his Master.

Arraign for judgment your social practices, your ambiguous excuses, your timid evasions, your weak anxiety to be on the safe side, your dread of being sneered at, or laughed at, or left out of a "set," your shirkings of responsibility, your hiding from a public duty and calling it modesty, your halting resolution, your shameful assents to calumnies, your silence where silence is falsehood or treachery, the smile on your face when there is protest, or reproof, or contempt in your heart. What are the Forty

Days for if not for this? The hackneyed lists of sins in the manuals and directories and confessionals need to be extended. What would happen if the men and women who have taken vows of loyal allegiance to Christ in the Church should go into a modern evening party, or even stand at the gate of the Lord's house, saying, as Joshua, the typical Hebrew hero, said to the man he met at Jericho, "Art thou for us, or for our adversaries?" In all the companies of noble spirits saved in Heaven, as among the groups that Dante saw when he walked in Paradise, there will be none nobler than those of whom it can be said, "These are they who on the earth were not afraid."

The prime minister of fear is compromise. Let worldliness become a little religious, and religion a little worldly, let self-indulgence talk the language of the Church and the Church borrow the wardrobe of the world, let the respectable thieves of the stock market be seen and heard at the conference and prayer-meeting, let partakers at sacraments waive their scruples and be "liberal," let luxury and materialism, extortionate monopolists, .despots of mine and factory, and robbers of work-women say the Creed and pay the pew-tax,—then may not the Gospel and mammon dwell peacefully together, then may not courage be dropped out of the catalogue of Christian virtues? A conscience that will not compromise, a steady, unyielding bravery for God, for the righteousness of God, for the truth of God, for the rights and liberties of every son and daughter of God, however undefended or poor,—is this a characteristic of our American, republican, nineteenth century Christian life?

Count up, then—it will humiliate us, but humiliation is Lenten business—the hindrances that put back truth, and justice, and charity, and a thousand blessed reformations in the world, from cowardice. What losses God's kingdom suffers, not now from hatred, or cruelty, or lust, or avarice alone, but from their vulgar ally, cowardice! Society is the wide, sad council-chamber of the rulers where, every hour, by some recreant affection or fugitive virtue, afraid of His righteousness, Christ is betrayed. Watch it. See the retreating and hesitating, the trimming and apologizing, the pale signals of fainting manhood in the countenance, the vanquished confidence in the eye, the sinking independence in the tone, the truth half-told, and the other half stifled by a sudden dread, the draggled flag of defeated magnanimity flying from the field.

Some wrong is on the eve of being righted, some suffering neighbor's pain or poverty might be relieved, some slander crushed, some injured reputation vindicated; a nobler thought is born in some bright mind which would grandly set forward the brotherhood of men, the reign of love, the gospel of life; but close after the divine idea comes an instigation of the earth earthy; of self selfish; of the devil devilish. What will the world say? How will this bear on my interest, my income, my prospects of promotion, my favor with the patron, the partisan, the customer, the voter, the rich parishioner, the influential family, the profitable patient, the desirable client, the social leader, the ruling majority? A generous impulse springs to life in the heart; but before it comes out to a hearty utterance on the lips or is embodied in a deed, fear kills it with a crafty calculation. And this is our horrible slaughter of the innocents, the nobler children of our humanity, murdered by Herod, lest Christ should live.

Most of these degraded timidities in our average Christian come not from absolute malignity, like Herod's, but from feeble principles and confused perceptions of where the two ways part. We are not quite sure whether this man with the drawn sword is for Christ or for his adversaries, and we are afraid to ask him. O, if only the two kingdoms stood out over against one another with plain lines and contrasted colors, like white and black, how much easier duty would be! There is so much in the world's amiabilities and industries, its winning ways and elegant arts, that seems to be good; and there is so much in the Church's bigotry, and controversy, and pharisaism, and moral bitterness that is certainly morbid and deformed! We think we shall get hard-headed men and frivolous women to sacraments and penitence by going half-way with them to Babylon. We undertake to make religion popular by making it less and less religious. We propose to be "liberal" by giving away what it is not ours to give, God's truth. We want the world's money for the Gospel, and so make the Gospel every day less and less worth anybody's money, or anybody's enthusiasm, or confidence, or zeal. We imagine we shall conciliate to the Church the spirits of darkness, not considering what a church with such spirits for supporters, preachers and singers must be. So far as we know there was never a people on the earth really honoring cowards. While Christ is Master, disciples who are afraid to face His enemies and bear His cross not only cannot share His triumph, they cannot know what His triumph is.

"Why haltest thus, deluded heart?
Why waverest longer in thy choice?
Is it so hard to choose the part
Offered by Love's almighty voice?
O look with clearer eyes again,
Strive thou to enter not in vain.
Press on!

"Remember 'tis not Cæsar's throne,
The proud world's honor, wealth or might,
Where God's high favor shall be shown
To him who conquers in this fight.
Himself and His eternity
Of life and joy He offers thee.
Press on!"

ALMIGHTY God, our only strength in mortal frailty, teach us ever to value Thy love above all things, and to esteem Thy favor more than life itself; and grant that we may pass through all the temptations of this world with peace, and innocence, and safety. Enable us to fight manfully against our great adversary, who is daily lying in wait to destroy us.

Suffer us not, O merciful God, to be led away by the vain and foolish customs of this world, nor seduced from our duty by the company and example of wicked men: but grant that we may fearlessly make Thy laws the rule of all our actions; and let it be our constant and most zealous endeavor to please Thee above all things in the several places and stations wherein Thy Providence is pleased to place us. Grant this, through Jesus Christ, our Lord. Amen.

Fourth Wednesday.

COURAGE.

THERE is no more need to construct an argument in behalf of courage than an argument for beauty, or health, or fresh air. Mankind, civilized and savage, having agreed in admiring it, if Christians as Christians, if the Church as a Church, do not make it manifest in their life and use it for their cause they fall below the common level of humanity. What it concerns us to consider is its nature, how it is nourished, how a consecrated will courts it and depends upon it for the building of character. We shall honor it the more the better we know the moral ingredients that make it up.

Men are indifferent to danger when they believe in something that is greater than themselves, higher, larger, worth more than their own comfort. Swiftly, as by a divine instinct, they put that greater thing first; it is easy to let life, blood, comfort, go for it. There is no cautious process of comparison and calculation. The surrender of selfish safety is spontaneous and generally unconscious. That is the crown and the glory of the brave man. If he sacrifices the favor of his whole social class and alienates admiring friends by espousing an unpopular cause, taking ridicule or hatred or poverty instead, he has the valor because he believes in that cause and not in popularity. If in a moral crisis, when a question of right and wrong sharply divides a community, he breaks with old ties, disappoints his set, speaks the unexpected word or does the unfashionable thing, freely accepting the reproach of an "impracticable," or a traitor to his party that he may be true to a principle, his bravery is simply the unavoidable action of his faith; he believes in the principle; he does *not* believe in any safe surrender of it; and his hurt pride, his crushed ambition, his tortured sensibilities, his scanty income, are the sacrifice. They are the Gibeonites that Joshua made bondmen, "hewers of wood and drawers of water for the house of God." Just then the popular thing in Israel was to slaughter Hivites and Hittites. Joshua and his princes, for certain reasons, had promised these captives that they should not be slaughtered but kept alive. The congregation clamored. The courage wanted for radicalism yesterday is wanted to-day for conservatism. In place of the boldness of aggressive measures to exterminate an enemy, there is needed now the calm fortitude that spares him; and here it is, "We have sworn unto them, by the Lord God of Israel; now, therefore, we may not touch them." There was belief in a promise, and in God who keeps promises. It is true enough, there is a mere animal courage in some men which is born in the blood, an appetite for battles, an exultation in peril, which has made dashing warriors; it is no more Christian than the size of the hand or the color of the eyes; but that too is a kind of barbarous faith in the thing the man fights for, which makes him fearless; and the rule holds. In that purple and fine linen tyranny which rules the customs and courtesies of social life with weapons sharper than a sword, some Christian woman defies that despotism. She dares to be simple in style, to be economical, to be just, not to tempt her weaker sisters by admired displays, harmless to herself, which would be ruin to them:—she braves the world's laugh or sneer because she believes in character, in duty, in Christ. A soldier rides cheerfully into the valley of death because he believes in his country, his leader, his flag. And, remember, whenever fear paralyzes your tongue, or drives you into dishonor, or crowds you into unclean company, it is only because you *do not believe* in veracity, or purity, or honor. Peter loved his Master when he denied Him, but he was afraid. It was the same difficulty on the water. Christ said, "Wherefore didst thou doubt?" Slow of heart to believe, weak of heart to obey. Let us put, therefore, as the first and noblest element in courage, faith. In the peerage of heroes recorded in the eleventh to the Hebrews you find the faith and the courage, in their root, were one. We hear certain persons praised as having "the courage of their convictions." But the courage is *in* the conviction, or else the conviction is not worthy of its name. As the Church is really believing it will be brave.

Along with faith is constancy. A long war sifts out a few patient, enduring generals from a multitude of brilliant, eager adventurers, stars that rise and set in a short campaign. The Christian life is a long war, with no discharge. Intensity of feeling at the beginning, high-wrought emotions at conversion, are not the tests of a courageous discipleship. Brave words may be spoken; there may be dashes of duty; ardent pledges; occasional excitements that bring a brief refreshment to a discouraged ministry. But time comes and tries them all of what substance they are. God wants for His servants here those souls that choose for Him once for all, and for all time; that having ranged themselves on His side stay there; that having taken the Church for their House abide by its law; that having called Christ Master follow Him to the cross; that having made a good confession and an honest vow are faithful to the end How much of the proof of loyalty lies in that endurance! Silent, unpraised, unstimulated, unpretending endurance! Few lives attract attention beyond a very narrow circle; few careers raise a ripple that does not sink to the broad flat face of the waters in less time than it takes the human body to grow. Yet every spot in the whole wide field is a scene of conflict, and in all these houses and streets, every day, there is courage or cowardice for God,—in the conscience, in the will, in the tongue, in the life. Now that persecutions are past, inquisitions are impotent, and crusades absurd, the greater part of valor is in standing at our posts, bearing the suffering that is sent, returning evil with good, conquering ourselves. Great soldiers have said that it takes more courage to sit still under fire than to fight in the most fearful engagement. After Joshua had swung his sword up and down all Palestine, had set his feet on the neck of prostrate kings, in the quiet godliness of his old age he dwelt in Timnath-Serah, and there is nothing finer than the scorching, painful, faithful words he spoke to his people, as keen as the sword's edge, till he bound them by shame and honor to his God, and set up the great stone for a witness under the oak in Mount Ephraim. In the heart of true valor there is always tenderness. Who has been brave if not the early Christian martyrs of the Roman catacombs? Their royal tormentors with the ferocity of brutes joined the exquisite ingenuity of artists and inventors in cruelty. Yet on the stone slabs where they carved the names of their dead, and the peaceful symbols of their hope, the dove, the anchor and the ship, there is not one trace of malediction, or anger, or revenge.

Again, a criterion of courage is solitude. The trial that tests its quality separates man from the supports of human sympathy. A great part of our Lord's sacrifice was its loneliness. "Ye shall be scattered every man to his own, and shall leave Me alone." We never come quite close to Him till we show that utter independence of men. Just when He longed to draw and bind all hearts to Him, then He must be forsaken,—not more solitary on the mountain-top at midnight than in the multitude at noonday.

In all the personal confessions of the strong Apostle we see nothing more pathetic than his "No man stood by me." There has been splendid intrepidity in the shock of armies and in the storm of the siege,—the courage of action,—but not the highest after all. An eloquent voice at Oxford described the inspiration that comes, in Church and army, from the sense of being a member of a great host. A figure of it was found in the issuing of the brave troops on the eve of the battle of Solferino out of the forest-country where they had marched all day. Concealed in the wood no soldier knew the force of the movement of which he formed a part. At sun-rise, as the vast lines of battalions filed out into an open plain, the light fell on miles of burnished arms and glittering standards; every eye flashed and every cheek flushed at the magnificence of the spectacle, for the multitude was instantly conscious of its strength. Yes, no doubt. But there is a loftier and grander heroism than that. It is in the heroes that stand in common places and suffer single-handed, with no shout to cheer them, no ranks, no banners, no trumpets, nothing but *the light*, and none to look on but God. Can you go straight on in the road when there is something rougher than rocks and colder than ice, alone, for Christ's sake? Then the accommodating and bargaining compromises of a supple society or a cringing church will have no peace, because they will have no power, like yours.

"Everlasting, changing never;
Of one strength, no more, no less,
Thine almightiness forever,
All the same Thy holiness;
Thee Eternal,
Thee all glorious we possess!

"Ours must be a nobler story
Than was ever writ thus far;
Nearer to Thee would we venture;
Of Thy truth more largely share.
Raise us nearer,
To Thy pure and perfect day!"

"Did we in our own strength confide,
Our striving would be losing;
Were not the right Man on our side,
The Man of God's own choosing.
Dost ask who that may be?
Christ Jesus, it is He
Lord Sabaoth is His name
From age to age the same,
And He will win the battle.

"That word above all earthly powers—
No thanks to them—abideth.
The Spirit and the gifts are ours
Through Him who with us sideth.
Let goods and kindred go,
This mortal life also.
The body they may kill;
God's truth abideth still,
His kingdom is forever."

O LORD Jesus Christ, Who art ascended into Heaven, there to intercede for us Thy servants, grant us firm faith in Thine Almighty power; strengthen our hope in Thee, O Jesus, King, most wonderful, hear us, Thou Who hast triumphed most gloriously; and grant that we may so follow Thee now without fear, in patient toil and suffering, that, when Thou comest again to judge the world we may sit with Thee in heavenly places; through Thy merits, O Lord and only Saviour, Who with the Father and the Holy Ghost livest and reignest ever one God, world without end. *Amen.*

Fourth Thursday.

CHRIST'S HEROES.

CHRIST'S mastery over the human race appears in His influence on its standards of heroism. Savage or civilized men admire heroes. Their heroes are men such as they would like to be. Our admirations furnish our inspiration, such as it may be. In the historical development of greatness and of the idea of greatness the body comes first. The first great heroes were the hard fighters, strong wrestlers, swift runners. It is remarkable how tenaciously this deference to physical ability keeps its place in the most intellectual modern communities. Our bodies are familiar to us; we know their uses, resources, limits, and they furnish with least study the most convenient measure of what man can do. Their strength, skill, suppleness, endurance, are almost as conspicuous and general marks of distinction, on land and water, and even in seats of education, now in the games of America, as in the Greek Olympics; mental ambitions and emulations are more, but the struggle for bodily superiority is not much less. Intellectual eminence comes next, a step higher in the scale; and of that there are many grades, from the low selfish cunning of the huntsman, money-maker and selfish political trickster, to the kings of thought and capitalists of knowledge, inventors, prophets, instructors, artists, philosophers. Moral greatness, the conquest of self, the power of sacrifice, the glory of heroic godliness comes last and comes slowly. It comes perfectly in the Son of Man and Son of God, the Second Adam, the Saviour.

If there is something to be done dangerous to the outward man, so hard that most people shrink from it and make excuse, something like rowing a boat among breakers to a sinking ship, or mounting to the top of a burning building to rescue a child, or entering a house where there is pestilence—then everybody says the prompt, strong oarsman, climber, nurse, is a hero. Suppose the peril and the daring were different, to risk reputation for righteousness, to give up party for principle, success for truth, property for honor, to speak unpopular words, to refuse and denounce a fashion because it is vicious or tempting, to take a stand which would make those whose love or favor we long for hate us, or those whom it would be for our interest to please angry with us. Here is another test of courage, a different measure of greatness, a new standard of heroism. Is not this precisely what Christ meant when He spoke to the world as its Master, and told us what we must do and be if we would follow Him?

It is very much the way of those who seek to stimulate their hearers or pupils to a nobler style of living, to set before them the examples of the great, and they are apt to find those examples in conditions so removed from the ordinary lot, so singular in original genius, in exceptional gifts, or in illustrious circumstances, as to take them out of the range of common comparison, sympathy, and even aspiration. They point to these signal instances of lofty achievement, celebrated in the Bible or memorable in history, inspired perhaps as prophets, or evangelists, or apostles, heroic missionaries, heroic reformers, saints whose heads are encircled with a nimbus of glory, as patterns to be imitated. And then the obscure toilsman, the diffident housewife, the timid beginner in the hard up-hill struggle, make their silent, discouraged answer: "What is all this to the needs and failures of a common heart like mine? It is all very well for you to glorify these splendid lives, and to tell us we, too, ought to be heroes and saints. But what is it that you expect of us.? Here we are in a commonplace age, an ordinary community, homely houses, every-day drudgeries, and we are no better, or brighter, or wiser, or stronger than the average. To-morrow morning we have got to take our work up just where we lay it down to-night. If you can help us there, we are very glad; but do not expect us to be famously virtuous, or transcendently devout, or heroic in the eyes of our neighbors, or memorable in the years to come. It will be quite as much as we can do to get through this fretting life decently, and be put into our coffins without disgrace. Preach to us as we are. Show us what the faith and the Church can do for us in our actual condition; and make us better if you can."

Very well, then, our Divine Master meets us exactly on that ground, and we ought to be willing to meet Him there. He never tells us to be like the great men of the world, the geniuses, the prodigies, the famous, the mighty, the men of learning or reputation or "success." He sets us no examples among the Pharisees, Scribes or rulers. He simply places Himself by our side, and shows us a perfect life, God's life on earth in man, and He says, "You are to be saints and heroes, every one of you, in the only true sense, just where you are. That is the reason why I have come to you where you are." He uses no compulsion, no violence. He does not put His power in the place of your liberty. Whoever lives the heroic or saintly life will do it of his own choice, his free will. There is no manhood, womanhood, character otherwise. Every person here can do it if he will. Your age, your social position, your sex, your business, your past life, the people you live with, have no controlling voice in this grand decision. To live with the Master, to live like Him, to live for Him, to help some one near you to live so, this is royalty, this is sanctity, and this is what the King of kings and the great High Priest means when He tells the least of His followers that they may be kings and priests unto God.

"By the old aspirants glorious,
By the brave hearts hoping all,
The believers made victorious,
In the Faith heroical;
By Thy dearest,
By Thy Samuel and Thy Paul,

"By their holy, high achieving,
By their visions more divine,
By each gift of our receiving,
From these mighty ones of Thine;
By the Spirit's word unspoken,
By Thy Truth as yet half-won,
By each idol still unbroken,
By Thy will yet poorly done.
Hear us, hear us,
Mighty Leader, lead us on!"

O GOD, Who hast made all those that are born again in Christ to be a royal and priestly race, grant us both the will and the power to do what Thou commandest; that Thy people who are called to eternal life may have the strength of faith in their hearts, and the courage of piety in their actions; through Jesus Christ our Lord. *Amen.*

Fourth Friday.

WILLING SACRIFICE.

In the primary signification of the word "sacrifice" there is involved an idea of a conflict between opposite claims, or affections; a conflict that carries with it suffering, and, when it results in the performance of the sacrificial act, costly to the doer, in his interests, his tastes, or his person. Where this meaning holds, the amount of reluctance in the sacrifice, in any line of religious conduct, will bear an inverse relation to the spiritual elevation and purity of the person pursuing it. What it costs one of us the pain of a hard struggle to surrender, another, whose mind moves in a more habitual and complete harmony with the mind of Christ, gives up with little feeling of loss and scarcely a consciousness of effort. When the stronger and larger part of our life and love is already on Christ's side, so that the first choice is for Him, then whatever He asks, either in the service of His Church, or in personal obedience, will be loosened and let go so cheerfully that there will hardly be enough of selfish reluctance left to calculate the cost. It is in this deeper and finer sense that sacrifice may be said to be the vital principle of the Gospel of Christ. Where this is not Christ cannot be, in any heart, in society, in the Church. It is of this willing pain and loss that the crucifixion is the supreme instance, the cross the sign, Friday the weekly memorial, and the redemption of the world, the fruit. Till we see the meaning of that deep mystical saying of the Saviour, "He that loseth his life for my sake and the Gospel's shall save it," we have apprehended neither the true glory and blessedness of our life nor the heart of the Gospel. It humiliates us to consider that we fret and complain at hardships which maturer Christians, whose discipline has been deep, whose vision is made clear, and whose unceasing alms and holy prayers have so come up for a memorial before God as to lift their own inward frame up into heavenly places in Christ Jesus, would instantly pronounce no sacrifices at all, but rather the refreshments of their journey. The Church ought not even for a moment to forget that just in whatever proportion her life rises into its true and honorable "peace in believing," in the same proportion she will forget to count up her offerings, and will reckon those things which a half-secular Christianity would either worry about or boast of as losses *for* Christ, to be so much gain *in* Christ.

There are traces of this gradation in the shades of meaning given to this word in Holy Scripture. Through the several kinds of sacrifice enjoined in the Mosaic ritual and regimen, each one being suited to some particular feature of the soul's relation to God and His law, or some special spiritual necessity in the discipline of character, there is a pervading presence of this great principle,—that something of value should be taken out of that which a man calls and considers his own and be put completely away from him, for Jehovah's sake. The instinct of property must be crossed and crucified. Human ownership, and that absolute and entire dependence of man the creature on God the Creator which is only intensified by sin, leaving man literally nothing that is strictly his own, are utterly distinct conceptions. Practically they are contradictory and antagonistic. Ownership, therefore, both in the Jewish Church and the Christian Church, must be abandoned or transmuted into stewardship. Man holds temporarily what he gathers from the earth, or earns by his faculties, *in trust* for his Lord, whose the earth is, whose plan it is to make the earth itself a mere building-place for His divine kingdom, and who comes to reckon. To keep this fundamental idea alive in the mind, and in fact to turn it from an idea of the mind into a living faith of the soul, is one of the objects of the system of sacrifices. While men are allowed to handle and manage, to a certain limit, what they are also permitted, in a kind of figure, to call their property, as a part of the discipline of their moral liberty,—to try and prove them what manner of men they are,—they are also continually to be opening their hands and parting with this substance, putting it clean away from them, cost what it will, laying it on altars, burning it in the fire, beating it small, scattering it as incense on the air, making it the maintenance of the Lord's Priesthood, sending it away into the wilderness. It is striking, too, that this system is made so pliant and accommodating as to the amount of the trust held, even in the rubrical exactness of it, that he that hath much shall give plenteously and he that hath little gladly give of that little,—the small store of the peasant, like the Virgin Mother of Him who, though He was rich, became poor for our sakes, being neither wholly excused nor yet burdened, but yielding its two turtle-doves or young pigeons. Beyond the tithe of all income for holy uses there must be these constantly recurring acts of costly surrender of earth to Heaven, self-will to God's will, appetite to a neighbor's comfort, property to infinite love. There is both the reality of a particular sacrifice and the symbolism of a universal submission, where everything is confessed to belong to the Lord. Thus the idea of merit is radically and logically excluded. The Evangelists are folded up in Leviticus. Suppose Jew or Christian gave everything he has and is to his Maker, in hands unstained and with sinless heart, still he would have done only what it was his duty to do, and be a servant without profit. And when the deep-struck, all-contaminating sin, in man's blood and his will, has added robbery to unprofitableness, there must be not only sacrifices of expiation for this uncleanness and transgression, but underneath all their inadequate atonement must lie the solemn covenant-prophecy, the anticipated propitiation of the Lamb of God, "not without" more precious "blood," sufficient, final, everlasting in redemptive power, rendering even the offerings of Christian worship dependent on the offering of the cross, as the altar of incense was united with the altar of sacrifice. "The fire shall ever be burning upon the altar; it shall never go out."

What a melancholy commentary it is on the wretched conceits of a mere spontaneous, impulsive religious condition, that wherever these two things are forced apart,—where almsgiving is divorced from the faith of the cross, charity is attempted without the atonement, the Lord's poor cease to be supplied from the Lord's altar, the offertory is lost out of its Scripturally appointed place beside the sacrifices of prayer and praise, and the people refuse to lay by on the first day of the week as the Lord hath prospered them; there, sooner or later, the effect appears in the alienation of the poorer class from the sanctuary; in the destruction of the sense of sacred responsibility for wealth on the part of the rich; in the substitution of spasmodic appeals for "causes" instead of steady persuasions for the one great blessed Cause, the Church which embraces all other causes, and for Christ's dear sake; in eloquent exaggerations and public subscriptions so devised as to drive men into seeming to give God handsome sums which are actually paid to "buy themselves off from a reputation for meanness" with their neighbors; in the secularizing of charity and the paganizing of philanthropy; in the vulgarities of fairs and exhibitions and their attendant moral humiliations,—the very purpose of which is to hide out of sight and to kill out of the soul that central reality of sacrifice which is the giving up to the Lord of that which *costs* the selfish heart something.

Intermixed, however, with these searching and inspired doctrines and ordinances of religious sacrifice we find in the Bible, as if intentionally put there to sustain the view already advanced, viz., that they who begin in the divinely-appointed path and keep on in it will presently find their costly offerings becoming joyous rather than grievous,—such expressions as the "sacrifices of thanksgiving," the "sacrifices of praise," and "sacrifices of joy." If there is any paradox it clearly belongs to that grand paradox which runs all through the Gospel and its transforming work; the "service that is perfect freedom"; "as poor yet making many rich"; "having nothing yet possessing all things." That is, if the Church would fill out her rightful office, restore the waste places, and extend the kingdom of Christ in the world, she must restore first the divine plan of faith working by love which God gave her; she must re-affirm the doctrine of stated, systematic and adequate sacrifices for that holy end; she must not cheat her children with any delusive dream of putting the cloke of Christ's righteousness on themselves or others so long as the thick under-garment of their own selfishness and avarice clings close to them and is not rent apart and torn off; she must teach and train every child she baptizes to keep his eyes, his hands, his feet, and all his powers ever ready and intent to seek out and to occupy the occasions of self-denial for her honor and the glory of her crucified Head; and then it will come about, as the promises of God are true, under the wonder-working law of the spirit of life in Christ Jesus, that a *love* for this kind of service will grow up, and a sacred passion for the Church's honor will be kindled, such as will cast out the bondage of constraint, enthroning the gracious and royal law which is "ready to give and glad to distribute," making of each disciple the "cheerful giver" whom the Lord loves.

And remember that this spirit, not held off for a distant sentimental admiration but brought in and embodied in our lives, is a very homely, practical, every-day thing. It has place in any room of the house, from morning till night. It is in the little and continual givings up of what is pleasant, in such quiet skilful ways of holy ingenuity, loving contrivance, and blessed thoughtfulness, that they for whom the sacrifice is so secretly borne shall never know what was suffered for them,—in which veil of reserve the beauty of the act so often lies, the beneficiary seeing nothing but the bright and spontaneous cheerfulness of the favor, and not even knowing perhaps what it cost or whence it came ;—and then the act is no longer small, but rises into the greatness of the honor of the cup of cold water given in the name of a disciple under the benediction of Christ. There is no comfort, no delight, no social indulgence or play, no domestic advantage or luxury, no first place of rest, or enjoyment, or eminence, but it may be turned and transfigured by the youngest person into one of these nobler offerings to the Lord Jesus, and so beautified with the sign of the cross.

"Lord, one deep trouble of my soul,
From which I pray to be set free,
Is that I cannot self control
And give up all the world for Thee.

"My weak, corrupt, deceptive heart,
Whenever early lusts I flee,
Like Ananias, yields a part,
But will not give up all for Thee.

"Sapphira like, false thoughts arise
When, penitent, I bend the knee
To hold the world before mine eyes
And say I gave it all for Thee.

"Lord, make me victor in the strife!
Thou who hast given so much for me
Teach me this parable of life,
That I have *naught* to give for Thee!"

O LORD Jesus Christ, give us grace to receive from Thy hand whatever pains and sorrows we endure in the flesh or in the spirit as so many portions of Thine own cross given unto us by Thee for the purifying of our souls, bearing every loss and trial with Thy patience, and rejoicing to suffer with Thee, for Thy sake who didst suffer and die for us, who yet livest to make intercession for us, now and ever. *Amen.*

Fourth Saturday.

WHY CAST DOWN?

Is not something like this true? You entered on a Christian life in the Church with an honest heart. It was your duty, and you did it. Probablv there was some struggle at the very outset. You took up a cross. But you hoped that after that, as you should go on, the cross would grow lighter, the way would open, your feet would get used to the road, and your shoulders be fitted to the burden. In this expectation you have been partly disappointed. The hard work, the hard places, the hard sacrifices, are in your path still, and you meet them every day. You are half disposed to complain. Your faith is disturbed. You ask whether the Church is what it professed to be, whether the religious life with God is what you took it for, whether your Lord who called you to come after Him is as good as His promise. You "think it strange concerning the fiery trial" which tries *you*, for we are always apt to think our own trials *are* "fiery," "as though some strange thing happened unto you."

Some one says, I am not satisfied with my religious progress. My Christian character is not what I want it to be, or what I expected it to be This conscience in me tells me I ought to be constantly gaining in goodness, overcoming my faults, becoming more and more like Christ my example, less worldly, less selfish, less petulant, more interested in my daily devotions, more constant and devout in enjoying my sacramental privileges, more thoughtful for others, more pure in heart. You told me if I came into the Church I should be able to go on from grace to grace; that Baptismal grace given me with the water at the font would make me clean; that Confirmation grace would make me strong to do my work; that Eucharistic grace at the Lord's Table would make me watchful, steadfast and peaceful. Time runs on and I do not find these fruits of the Spirit either ripening or multiplying in me. What is the matter?

Christ has taught His Church what to answer to this, and has written it in His Gospel. To be alarmed will probably do you no hurt; to be discouraged would be a fatal and faithless mistake. There is not one word of discouragement in the whole Gospel, from the beginning to the end. Your Father wants to save your soul, not to cast it out, and He will save you if you will let Him. Your willingness to let Him,—the name for that is faith. There are two or three short answers to this trial of despondency. Perhaps you are right as to the fact. You may have fallen back. You may have stood still. You may have gained in some virtues, and lost in others. One thing is certain, where you have really failed the fault is yours, not in Him who so loved you as to die for you. Keep on searching yourself till you find out what you have left undone. Did you suppose the baptismal water would not only wash your old sin away but that it would be an insurance against it in all time to come, an amulet to drive off bad spirits, even though you opened the door to them, a charm to protect you, though you went where you knew it was wrong for you to go? Did you imagine God's gift at Confirmation would disarm all your adversaries as well as put strength into your hands? Can you think that the consecrated food at the Supper of the Lord, while it nourishes your own secret life, will kill all temptations, within and without, though there is no regular and resolute action of your will to beat them down? No matter how rich the spiritual gift from Christ may be, unless you stir it up and use it in well-doing it perishes, as the grass and grain in all the fields will spoil if you pack them away green out of the air and light. God never bestows a talent to be rolled up and hid. You accuse yourself of indifference at your prayers, or apathy at church. Do you take pains about them, prepare for them, think over beforehand what special things you need to ask for yourself or for those you love, or what mercies you have received to be thankful for? You had a bitter resentment against an acquaintance, a grudge burning in your breast, and you hoped your religion would cool it away. Did you give your religion a chance by banishing self-justifying thoughts, by burying the wrong and never bringing it to life, by forgiving even seven times? Take care not to blame the religion of Christ for shortcomings or backslidings which that religion warned you against when you began.

It may be, however, that you are mistaken. We are not always the best judges or fair critics of our own spiritual frame. There is an illusion of the eyes on a railway train or in a boat on the river where we fancy we are sitting still and everything about us is in motion, when really it is the other objects that are still and we are moving. There are morbid moods of the soul, as there are disordered states of the body, and sometimes the last create the first. At any rate, if you see your own defect and deplore it, that of itself is the very sign of kindling life, and you have a right to draw not self-satisfaction but hope from it. Penitence is the first movement to mercy, and confession to God is the first step upward. Were you satisfied with self that would be death; pain is the evidence of vitality, the outcry and alarm-bell of the sinning conscience. Take heart from it. The holiest saints on earth and in Paradise have had a poor sense of their own advancement. In the awful depth of agony at His passion our blessed human Lord cried out with something very like discouragement. The true way to get comfort is to look away from yourself to Him. Our power, our light, our satisfaction, our better life itself, are in Him, and to Him we must go, and go again and again for them, not to ourselves. God grant us just discontent enough with what we are to stir and nerve us for harder and nobler labor, not so much as to depress our energies or darken our daylight! The best reply you can make to your reproachful memory, charging you with meagre attainments and slow progress, is that you will stop measuring yourself by yourself, drop the bad habit of prying about in the interior of your own weak heart for satisfaction which can come only from a higher source. Look unto the hills of God, whence comes your help, and forgetting the things which are behind reach on to better things before.

"What is it makes my feet so tired and sore?
Is it from running swift to do His will,
Or from a long, hard chase for glittering drops,
That I my cherished treasure-cup may fill?

"Hands weary! Is it from the tears they've wiped,
Or pointing many to the living way?
Or are they weary gathering flowers that fade,
Or grasping joys and hopes which will not stay?

"Whence doth this grief and disappointment come?
Is it that men will put my Lord to shame,
Or has proud self been overthrown and balked
In some dear plan for ease, or love, or fame?

"O, self has been my end, my aim, my god!
No wonder that I cry for rest and peace!
But dare I hope the heavenly rest to gain
When wearied out in such a cause as this?

"O let me turn and learn to prize my life
Because for Jesus I may spend it all;
And count the longest, hardest life but short,
And all my grief and sorrow light and small!

"Then, when I've labored through the heat and cold,
And brought my sheaves in patience to His feet,
Then may I lay my head upon His breast,
And know the laborer's rest so full and sweet."

BE near, O Lord, to us who call upon Thee; and forasmuch as Thou dost chasten us with disappointment and heal us by smiting, and make us strong by removing our confidence from ourselves and placing it only in Thee, grant that we may accept this Thy Fatherly correction, and be turned by it into the path of a thankful obedience to Thy commandments, and trust in Thy forgiving love, through Jesus Christ our Lord. *Amen.*

Fourth Monday.

THE MULTITUDE FED.

WHATEVER the reason for setting the account of our Lord's kindness to the bodily want of five thousand people as the Gospel for the middle of Lent, there is no question what can be learned from it, or that it suits our modern life and habit of mind in society and in the Church.

See, first, how the simplicity of the action works itself into the style of the narrative. Simplicity is one of the surest marks of truth. It is only when we get out of nature into criticism, which is apt to be first self-conscious, then artificial, and then skeptical, that there is a doubt that everything happened on that hillside just as it is told. Something is about to be done such as has not been seen or heard of before. Imagine yourself one of the five thousand,—no regular meal since day before yesterday, none at all to-day. There lie the five barley loaves of the common size and the "two small fishes." How do you think a professional wonder-worker, a Simon Magus, any pretender, would have gone about his prodigy? How would fiction, or the stage, or a partisan historian, a Victor Hugo, the poet who never loses sight of his reputation, the enthusiastic biographer, magnifying his hero and himself together, would have wrought that description which, for fifty generations of men, was to be read with reverent faith? Five thousand hungers satisfied; five thousand faces looking in amazement at one another; five thousand pairs of eyes seeing half a bushel of wheat, without planting, or harvesting, or flail, or winnowing-fan, or flour-mill, grow into the feast which becomes a vast sacrament of charity, and yet not a syllable of astonishment put into the record by these sure witnesses. What does this simple, straightforward style mean? It means that these men were too full of the unspeakable reality to cry out, "Lo, here," or "Lo, there." Let alone the authority of inspiration. Not till the laws of intellectual life are reversed, not till students of language forget its profoundest principles, can they make impostors out of these evangelists. Nature is true to nature, answers to herself, testifies to herself, in a crystal, a song of a thrush, a human voice, or a Gospel. It sounds unprofessional, perhaps, but I feel sure that if these New Testament biographies of Christ had been left more to themselves, if theologians had been less anxious to vindicate them, if their intrinsic majesty and serenity had been let alone by ecclesiastical door-keepers and apologists, if Christ Himself in the tenderness and glory of His divine humanity had been made the immediate object of faith and the living light of His Church rather than this or that piece of external evidence about Him,—then men would have seen that His supernatural acts were really as natural to Him as anything in His life; that His miracles were the necessary outcome of His power and His love, because now and then He could not otherwise accomplish his gracious purposes, or express Himself so well; that it was just what was to be expected that there should be openings around Him of that higher and more resplendent world out of which He must have come; that in fact it would have been strange and unnatural if, when ordinary things would not serve His loving purpose, the extraordinary should not obey Him—the winds and the sea, disease, dumbness, death—and so here that the loaves and fish should not be made to fill the fainting multitude as never before, and the small grow suddenly great in His almighty and all-merciful hands.

When I think of *what He was*, even the shining garments of His Transfiguration appear to me as fitting raiment for Him as the every-day dress He wore in the cottage at Nazareth or Bethany.

So much for the fact. Our Lord's superhuman work and our own best human sense of it agree. The farther we explore them the more the spiritual and the intellectual laws harmonize. When a great company who had been listening to the Master's good news from Heaven were hungry, nothing was more likely than that the Master would have "compassion on them." The food He had fed their nobler part with was really as miraculous as the bread, and the one as suitable as the other. When God's children wanted a knowledge of their Father more than they wanted anything else, what so probable as that God's elder Son would come and reveal Him?

Sometime or other, when our human race has grown more to its maturity, when science has become more scientific than it is yet by being more comprehensive, men will not be content to live wholly in the narrow limits of their material encampment, this little door-yard of a planet, but will see ampler and grander fields opening around them and above them, answers to thoughts in them that wander through eternity, and will be persuaded that when the Son of God is on His errand of unmistakable love what is to us a miracle will be as likely to take place as our seed-time and harvest. When education is complete, the whole material universe will be a symbol and a type of what eye cannot see and the ears cannot hear. The perishable and the eternal will be one.

Come next to the *motive* of the miracle. Certainly it was not to astonish a superstitious crowd. Christ's heart lies as open as the landscape to the light. First in His thought always is the first want in His neighbor. There is the secret of His supremacy; this is the heart of this new kingdom which has come and gained the faith of the world. This ought to be the central thing, the essential thing, in the creed and the worship of the Church. "I have compassion on the multitude, for they have nothing to eat." The Church must learn it again, and, as fast as it unlearns it, learn it again and again. Here is its doctrine, and its practical business. In comparison with this regeneration of the race by the wonder-working power of Love, any special wonder is only an incident or an instrument. To make a few sick people well, to heal ten lepers, to liberate a poor frame bent double with rheumatism, is a symbol. It illustrates the boundless charity of a Saviour. If we turn that bounty of the bread, or the blessing of giving back to the sisters at Bethany their dead brother to be with them a few years more and then die again, or the quieting of a storm for a boat's crew on a lake, if we turn this merciful and beautiful ministry of miracle into the substance of His religion, or make the religion itself dependent on such evidence, we blunder terribly. "Blessed are the pure in heart," "I am the Light of the world," "He that humbleth himself shall be exalted," "Come unto Me and I will give you rest,"—how can any one of these immortal and undeniable sayings be the more true for the restoring of a withered hand? This is Christ's own explanation of His miracles. *Come* to Me, He says, for what I am, and because I came forth—God's life incarnate—from God the Father. Believe in Me because I give Myself for you. Be gathered into My Church because *I* am there, and there you shall learn My will, be trained in My school, get holy habits, take sides with My peaceful army, commune with Me at My table. You shall help on this slow conquest of sin. You will not find everything even here in the Church in divine order; the Church on earth will not correspond altogether to its heavenly pattern; the visible body of Christ will not include all of His Spirit, because men and women who enter it are both faulty and weak, and they bring in with them their manifold infirmities. The Church is Mine, He says, I love it, and gave Myself for it; you, if you are wise, will love it, and give yourselves to Me and to one another in it, and so live as to make it what it ought to be, "without spot or wrinkle." My healings and feedings of your bodies point you to a deeper cure, a larger salvation; a richer and more nourishing Eucharist. They are means, not an end; secondary, not first; signs, not the substance. He said, Believe Me for what I bring and offer to your souls; but if you will not, then believe Me for the work's sake; see what the sign signifies, and lay hold of that. There is something like a tone of rebuke: "Except ye sees signs and wonders ye will not believe." These miracles are accommodations to your dulness, condescensions to your low estate. Open your eyes and see. If you will not or cannot welcome the glorious and loving revelation I offer you in My sacrificial pleading and prayer, in My Sermon on the

Mount, in My agony, My tears and blood, and the patience of My cross, I will be patient still; here is medicine for your aching or fevered flesh: here is the touch of My hand, the hem of My garment, the five loaves and two fishes; let them satisfy you as to who I am, and why I am come. Only let me lead you, and bear your children on My shoulders. No doubt some of you will have to come from a far country; no matter, it is coming homeward; "divers of them came from far." Come any way, by any road, drawn by the cords of Heaven or by the cords of a man. You are heavy-laden; you labor with dissatisfaction; you are discontented in your unbelief; you are not very successful in your work, and are disappointed; you are not very wise, and least wise when you imagine you are; you are misunderstood; you have heart-aches that are not to be told. The hunger is in your soul. Then *you* are one of the "multitude." They are *more* than five thousand. I have compassion on them all. You and they all, unless you are refreshed, will "faint by the way."

People keeping Lent, or going to a mission, are told in the churches that there are seven deadly sins. So there are, and seventy times seven sins that in your hearts and lives will kill your spiritual life if you do not fight day and night, Sundays and week-days, against them. But we do not find in the ordinary list one which Christ our Master, who knows us through and through, puts always among the first. This sin is the daily breaking of one-half of that two-fold commandment where He sums up the whole law, which, if you mind it, makes you a Christian and gives you everlasting life: "Thou shalt love thy neighbor as thyself." We go around that to make sure of our own comfort. We leave it out. We hurry it over. We hide it under doings and preachings that do not strike us so hard and cut so deep.

The miracle of the loaves cuts deep. The meaning of it is Lenten food.

"From feasts that perish turn aside
A little space,
O be the flesh indeed denied;
Our souls an-hungered satisfied
With the sweet feast of grace

"Thou who didst fast so long, so sore,
For our poor sake,
All pangs of earth's vast hunger bore,
Ere thou Thy precious blood didst pour,
Thy blessed body break.

"O Holy Jesus! hear our cry,
And give us strength,
For love of Thee to mortify
The love of self till self shall die,
And leave us Thine at length!"

O GOD, Who art Love, and Who makest men to be of one mind in an house, grant to Thy children who eat of thy Heavenly Bread to bear one another's burdens in the good will of a perfect charity, and in service to one another's necessities, that Thy peace, which passeth all understanding, may keep our hearts and minds in Jesus Christ our Lord. *Amen.*

Fourth Tuesday.

WHO ARE YET TO BE FED?

It is a distinct aspect of the miracle of the multiplied loaves, and of weighty meaning when great multitudes are hungry, that it represents the Master of men as their Feeder. What is it that we see on the mountain-side? The Strong One serves the weak. The high-born, eternally-begotten of the Father, passes the dishes to the poor. The Lord of all the fields where the grain grows, of all the seas where the fishes swim, is a working-man. The only actual landlord on earth collects no rent, demands no tax, is not waited upon. He thinks, cares, labors, for them that have "nothing to eat." Our question is, Has the meaning of this miracle expired? Because you and I, between house and shop or field, along streets where we walk or drive, at the doors of our churches, see no multitude having literally "nothing to eat," has the object lesson in Galilee no application here? Because He who broke the bread there has gone to that Heaven to which He lifted up His eyes and gave thanks, have we no calling to be feeders in His name and to make His Church a brotherhood? Then why does the Church keep this record in her Prayer Book, and three times a year put it, or its equivalent, on the lips of her children? What do modern congregations believe St. Paul meant when he wrote to Christians that the Son of Man, "though He was rich, became poor"? Did he mean that being rich Christ made it His business to become richer and richer,—richer by merciless competition with His neighbors, richer by buying cheap and selling dear, richer by taking every possible advantage of other men's ignorance or misfortune, richer by joining a ring, or consolidating a monopoly, or manipulating a market, or paying working-women a fifth part of what their work is worth, or renting tenements at twenty per cent profit where fever and filth and vice go with the lodging,—richer by any game that money itself, or a sharp brain, or a cruel hand, can play? Emptying our Lord's words of the original sense that He put into them, His orders, His warnings, is no part of a Christian prophet's business; yet it is this very thing, done from favor, from fashion, from cowardice, that keeps the consciences of a great many men and women, who say the Creed and respond to the Ten Commandments, comfortable. The two kingdoms which Christ sundered and held apart, declaring that no man can serve both at the same time, are as irreconcilable now as they ever were. The Son of Man came on earth to give; are most of us living to give, or living to get? Are we Christ's people then? You may fancy that in a prosperous republic the line that separates class from class has been blotted out or blurred over. But no; in most congregations it is as sharp though not so visible as in the fashions and parlors of society. The better part of the world and the worse part of the Church conspire to accommodate the two together, with this result, that the world pays a pew-tax to the Church, and the Church, in its financial policy, its estimate of preaching, its hunt for popularity, its passion for display, is more and more like the world. How many parishes are conducted on the plan of giving the Bread of Heaven to those who have none of it to eat? How many churches are built in compassion for those who are far off from the Father's House? How many of us, individuals, in our personal following of Him who gave Himself for us, think first, as He did, or work and give and pray with Him, for those, near or far, who have not our privileges, our comforts, out strength or light,—some share with us of the things that are best in the world,—or our easy access to satisfactions higher and nobler than these?

We take our comfort, perhaps pride, in our Church and its worship. But Christ our Lord will not have us separate this mystical Body from the deeper mystery of our personal life. What pathetic delusions the decorations all are if they hide from us the preciousness of the poorest, meanest, weakest heart of any son or daughter of the present infinite God. Look at the sights if you will; admire them if you know what they signify. But take care to turn and look *from* them to one of these souls that you neglect or despise outside your door, under the feet of your pride, God's immortal ill-clad child. A great European thinker and scholar, lately dead, a real and not a fictitious philosopher, living in his solitary chamber, apart from people but always living among the spiritual secrets which are the realities, writes this, one evening, in his diary: "The errand-woman has just brought me my letters. Poor little woman, what a life! She spends her nights in going backwards and forwards from her invalid husband to her helpless sister, and her days in toil. Resigned and indefatigable, she goes on without complaining till she drops." "Lives such as hers," he says, "prove something." "Ignorance that is deplorable is moral ignorance, that more vulgar ignorance in men and women who cannot read the alphabet of humanity, where the selfish misunderstand the self-forgetful, where luxury is blind to the beauty of simplicity, where culture misses the hidden romance and chivalry and tragedy in the grander theatre and holier gallery of living people everywhere." "The kingdom of God belongs not to the most enlightened, but to the best, and the best man is the most unselfish man." He might have said, the finest woman is the woman to whom she herself is least, and those that need her skill and graciousness, her smile and hand are first. "Humble, constant, voluntary sacrifice,—this constitutes the true divinity, the bond and charm of society," the light of all the rooms in a house, the strength and salvation of a state. "Without the worship of duty, without love of one's neighbor," without patient honesty, without religious "respect for law, the whole social fabric falls to decay. Neither letters nor art, neither luxury nor industry, neither the custom-house nor police," neither the splendor of public spectacles nor badges of fortune, can keep safe at last any structure of which the four foundations are not equity and charity, righteousness and truth. And therefore it is written, 'The last shall be first.'" And, as if that were not plain enough, "you that are first shall be last." "Society rests upon conscience not science," though science may build, and art adorn the edifice. Be not deceived; "Civilization is foremost and finally a moral thing. To every other architect one greater than any of them says, from eternity to eternity, 'Thou fool, *this night* thy soul shall be required of thee.'"

The Church is made by the Feeder of the people to be for Him a Feeder of the people. Not one of us but can bear a part in that beneficence and share in that glory, like the common men that handed the bread to the ranks on the hill, like the lad with the loaves. Who is the wiser man? He who in the meekness of his wisdom knows how to converse kindly not patronizingly, with the lowest; who stops in the race for money or knowledge to hear the story of wrong or misfortune, who brings the fruits of education or enterprise and spreads them before hungry minds; who opens paths of industry to the idle, the unskilful, the criminal; who pays not only wages but respect to laboring men or women, and refuses respect to them who do not; who does his best to refine heartless wealth with Christ-like tenderness; who summons shame and law together to emancipate pale children from the slavery of the factory and the mine; whose study it is

"How best to help the slender store,
How mend the dwellings of the poor,
How gain in life, as life advances,
Valor and charity more and more."

There are two feasts, both sacramental,—one at the memorial altar of the one Sacrifice made once for all; the other wherever Christ in His disciples toils, suffers, dies, for mankind.

"I stood outside, and looked within;
These banquet doors were flung full wide,
I saw my own heart stained with sin,
And Thy dear face, Thou Crucified!
The very hands that broke the bread
Bore nail-prints suffered once for us,
Thorn-marks upon the Sacred Head,
Thine arms outstretched, as on Thy cross!

"Out of my famished heart I cry,
'At last, at last, is this Thy House?
Feed me, my Saviour, even me,
With all these happy ones who come!

I have but tears to offer Thee!
  With this Thine holy feeding sweet,
I have no words! I "come and see,"
  And, hungry, kneel here at Thy feet!'"

BLESS, O Lord, we beseech Thee, all those who are devoted to serve Thee in works of charity, in the training of the young and reclaiming the fallen,—those who visit the sick, minister to the poor, instruct the ignorant, and lead back to the Father's House them that are astray. Accept their labors, and grant that while they sympathize with others in their necessity they may bring them to share the joy of the divine life wherein they live, may comfort the sorrowful with the consolation wherewith they are comforted of God, and may with them attain to that spiritual perfection which they desire, through the merits and mediation of our Saviour, Jesus Christ. *Amen.*

Fifth Wednesday.

THE MASTER THE INTERPRETER.

THE Master appeals to other parts of us than an underlying, inborn, unextinguished, undeveloped sense of righteousness, and even a latent desire for it. But He does appeal to that. If He did not His message would hardly be a Gospel, and it is not certain that He would have set up a kingdom of Heaven on the earth.

Yet we must face a sad fact; we must make a perplexing and mortifying admission against the credit of our human nature and kind. Some doubter will say, What if this high desire, this blessed aspiration, this passion for the living water does not burn in my heart, and the thirst for dead and dirty water does? The prophet hears it said back to him, with appalling frankness: "You tell me I must desire what I do not desire, and you tell me not to want what my senses and ambition and vanity *do* want,—the present pleasure, the fortune and equipage, the money in the bank, the style, the frolic, the "king's meat and the king's wine" for fashion is king, this world's "good time." How shall I begin to get me up to the higher and nobler and cleaner life? What shall attract and draw me to that other "well," deeper and older than Jacob's, the well you tell me of springing in the heart of Christ? Tell me this, or you mock me with a mirage of the desert, or a will-o'-the-wisp of the bog. You may keep on repeating from your pulpit, "Whosoever is athirst let him come," but you only tantalize me with the phantom of an imaginary joy, and I am as far off from your kingdom of Heaven as before."

But let us look a little closer. That Master who knew all that is in man and woman, in every bold man's and every yielding woman's heart, and needed not that any should testify, knows this about you too. He knows that your difficulty is not beyond His reach. To this end was He born, and for this cause came He into the world, that He might show you, uncover you, interpret you, to yourself. Are you sure that a *capacity* for a better life, after all, is not in you, and with the capacity some aspiration towards it; are you sure that the longing after loftier aims and purer affections, the friendship of God and the self-sacrificing charity of Christ, is really dead in you, or is it only smothered by your senses or hidden under rubbish or narcotized and paralyzed by the drugs and gases of a sorceress that has tempted you? Is it quite certain that never, at any time, anywhere, when you were alone, at night, when you have been sobered by bad news, or sickened, or disappointed, or betrayed, when you have seen the misery that your own folly or lust has created, or when you have been cheated by man or scorned by woman, when your plans failed or flesh ached, sure that never, anywhere, in any better hour, something said in you, I wish I were pure and right and true; I wish I were out of this bad, low, selfish way, for it gets lower and lower; I wish I were what I know I ought to be; I wish that God and I were friends, and that His candle shined upon my head? Well, *that* was the thirst. It came, but it did not stay. You had it, but you did not keep it. Worse yet, you did not ask God to satisfy it, and so you thirsted again, and you will thirst again and again, as your Lord told the woman, and the thirst will heat itself into a fire. You were wrong then when you said you were satisfied. You misunderstood, misjudged, abused yourself. Christ knew you better. Nobody is hopeless who admires goodness. Nobody is lost who wants to be saved. I have read the lives of many bad men and some bad women, for I have read history; and some of them I have seen. If men sunk so low and gone so far astray as St. Augustine and St. Ignatius before they were saints, and John Newton and John Bunyan and a host of other recovered and righteous souls all along, have turned from foul mud to "living water," leading many thousands up after them from the depths where they wallowed to the heights where they have ascended, then there need be no despair.

And so Christ becomes the great Interpreter of what we are. He comes to interpret us to ourselves. It is the first step towards the new and everlasting life. Christ does other things, and has other characters. He is Prophet, Priest and King. He is Sacrifice and Shepherd, Wine and Bread, Head of the Church and Intercessor at the throne. But that He may be all these to us He is to each and all of us first a Revealer of the secrets of the soul, as Simeon predicted He would be when He held Him in his arms at His birth. Not only does He reveal God to man; He reveals man to himself. It is so in some degree with all true prophets. They are listened to and followed by startled people and nations because they tell them something they had dimly felt in their own real inner life. Into whatever company Christ entered, the persons about Him had a new self-knowledge. Sometimes it angered them, as it did the Pharisees, or alarmed them, as it did Herod and Pilate. Sometimes it smote them into silence; sometimes it converted them. They went out, one by one, speechless, not gossiping or snarling any more at other people's sins, but astonished at the discovery of their own. He sifted out chaff from wheat, Scribes from Publicans, pretension from sincerity. Everybody's eyes were turned inward; each one saw how weak, or mean, or hollow, or selfish, or filthy he was, and how changed and cleansed and Christ-like he ought to be and might be. He said, Come to Me, and you shall have power to live out your better self, by the strength and inspiration I will give you. So He drew the world after Him; the common people heard Him gladly; only hypocrites hated Him; and the procession of His rejoicing and thankful followers has lengthened out from Sychar to the ends of the earth. Come to Him in your shame, and

He will lead you to honor and peace. Give Him yourself, and He will give you *back* to yourself transfigured, your manhood made complete like His, your womanhood made holy by His grace, your life made satisfying by your likeness to Him.

You ask still *how* He creates the thirst that brings you. In three ways He creates it. He does it first by lifting up before us the vision of good lives, far better than our own. You recall some face that you used to look at in your childhood where love and serenity and purity wrote out for you the living lesson and pictured for you the living beauty of holiness. Have you not known persons of whom you said, There is the embodied righteousness of Christ; there is Christianity *alive*, in a human shape and an every-day movement, in sweet temper, charitable speech, noble action. You read the biography of some saintly hero, and your heart kindles with a momentary sympathy. You take up your neglected New Testament, and there shines the marvellous splendor of that *one life of Love*, of which you know that you might have a blessed share in it, and have it more and more abundantly if you would. Perhaps you will say, Give me this, that I thirst not!

He does it, secondly, by conscience, that mighty

and awful witness within you which, in spite of all your levity and lying and unbelief, lives on, which survives through all the horrors and crimes and madness of our sinning race, which oceans cannot quench, and graveyards cannot bury, or earthquakes displace, because it is a part of humanity itself. It wakes up after you have drugged it to sleep. It comes back after you have driven it away. It is warning before you sin, commanding "Thou shalt not;" it is waiting by you while you sin, more faithful to you than you are to yourself; it is remorse and vengeance and agony after you have sinned,—afraid of your Father, ashamed of yourself, face to face with judgment. This *is* the thirst.

He does it, finally, by suffering. There is a fever, there is a restlessness, there is a pain, there is a deep disease, not of the body, and all of it in all the sorrowing world is made for good. It means amendment, repentance, prayer, newness of life. That is the key to every dark chamber. That is the interpretation of mysteries of sickness and mourning. That is the inmost sense of the Beatitudes of Him who knew when to hurt and how to heal. It is the undertone in the cry of your long days of grief, "Would God it were evening!" and of the longer nights, "Would

God it were morning!" It comes from shattered nerves, lost property, broken promises, unfaithful friendships, lacerated and lonely and speechless hearts. I needed what I would not seek, the deeper well. The earth under foot is not iron; the heavens overhead are not brass. God is not hard, or cold, or departed, or changed. My Christ has made bereavements beneficent, and crosses light, and pale faces beautiful, and all truth and goodness immortal, and every soul that comes thirsting to Him victorious over disorder and death. I am satisfied to be like Him.

Here we stop and think and pray. To-morrow, if we live till to-morrow, the march, the strife, the study, the trial will begin once more. We pray. What shall the prayer be? Whatever the other petitions for yourselves or those you love, pray this. You men who are not of the past but of to-day, you women who are not of Samaria but here, pray this, reaching out the hand of your faith: "Give me, O Master, this water, this glorious gift of God. Make me first to long for and then to live this life with Thee! Give it, or I shall never have it. It will not be wages, but bounty, for I shall never earn it. It will not be bought, for

" 'In my hand no price I bring.'

I beg it, for I am poor. I shall have it, for it is promised. I know Thee, Thou Traveller *once unknown*, in whom I have believed!"

" Thy life of sin has been
A toilsome path without one cheering ray;
Now on thy Father lean,
And He will guide thee in a better way,

" Come, leave the desert land,
And all the husks on which thy soul has fed;
And trust the faithful Hand
That offers thee a feast of living Bread.

"O sinner! 'tis the voice
Of One who long has loved and pitied thee!
He would thy heart rejoice
And set thee from all sin and suffering free."

O THOU with whom is the Fountain of Life, and in whose Light we see light, increase in us both the longing for Thy pardon and the brightness of Thy knowledge, that when we are thirsty we may receive refreshment from Thee, the Fountain of living waters, and when we are dark we may be enlightened and quickened by the clear shining of Thy countenance, O Saviour, Jesus Christ our Lord! *Amen.*

Fifth Thursday.

FALSE INTERPRETERS AND THE TRUE.

HERE we are, almost nineteen hundred years since One greater than Moses, with one breath of His lips swept away the transient cloud of glory from Gerizim and Jerusalem alike, and told *us*—you and me—how to find our Father. In all the religious disputes and faithless contradictions of the times, how shall any wayfarer find out that way? How shall one of these modern men, with his eyes and hands fastened on this world, and yet not quite willing to gain the world by losing his soul,—how shall one of these older people, seeing how fast life is slipping away and remembering how many times the forbidden apples that tasted sweet have turned to ashes in the mouth, awake and arise at the breaking of their dream, and be sure that they know in what and in whom they believe?

You will be met by four self-appointed guides, waiting at the corners of your streets, as blind every one as Bartimæus was before he was met by the Master and cried, "Jesus, thou Son of David, have mercy on me." They are a dogmatist, a sentimentalist, a sensualist, and a philosopher. One is a dogmatist. He offers you a handsome, clean-cut, hard and fast system of theological opinions, shaped and polished by human hands. You ask bread, and he gives you a stone. Another is a sentimentalist. He tells you to stir up your sensibilities, to catch the breezes of popular religious agitation, to run where the crowd runs, to answer shout with shout, to gaze at spectacular displays, to sing yourself into the kingdom, to get a religion of the emotions rather than of conduct, the religion that rouses feeling but forgets to settle and brace character. You wanted living water and he gave you froth. Another is a sensualist. He tells you to let alone your repentance and stop your prayers, to eat savory meat and crown your feast with roses and songs, to dress yourself at Vanity Fair and dance all night, till a voice wiser and stronger than his shall say, "Thou fool, *this* night thy soul shall be required of thee. You forsook the living well, and drank poisoned wine. The other is a philosopher. He tells you you have a brain and a stomach, but no soul; that your love for your mother, your friend, your father on earth or Father in

Heaven, is phosphorus; that history since the days of the Cæsars and Pontius Pilate is a lie; that all the liberty and learning and charity and anthems of Christendom for fifty generations are stamped with a false name, the name of a pretender who died for his pretence, a deceiver who lived in poverty and solitude and was crucified for His deception; that there is nothing in the universe but matter; that he has searched the starry heavens with his telescope and found no God; which is not strange, because telescopes were not made for seeing the invisible or measuring the Omnipresent; that he has opened the human skull with his scalpel and come upon no spirit there, which is very likely, for he looked in the wrong place; that the missionary heroism which, since some of our oldest men were born, has carried the Gospel round the globe, and translated it into a hundred and fifty dialects, and set the cross on all the continents and far-off islands of the sea, and finishes churches in this country at the rate of six every day,—is a kind of somnambulism; and that the Book which hundreds of millions of living and dying and thinking believers have clasped to their breasts because it showed them their Father's face and opened Christ's eternal House not made with hands to them, is an oriental fable or an exploded imposition. You asked for a hope of immortality, and your philosopher pointed you to a coffin and a grave.

Where then is the way? What is it to be a Christian? How shall I gain and live the everlasting life? Where shall I start? Go back to the well-stone Preacher at Sychar, and listen: "If thou knewest the gift of God, and who it is that saith to thee, Give me to drink, thou wouldst have asked of Him, and He would have given thee living water." The beginning of a Christian life, *i. e.*, is the taking of a gift, and the gift itself is a living, vital thing. But there will be no taking, no reaching out, no kneeling down at the fountain-head, unless first there is a want. I must be dissatisfied with what I am, and ashamed of what I have been. I must look long enough into my weak will and my faulty life, my temper, my selfishness, my appetite, my pride, my worthless habits and my unclean heart,—long enough and honestly enough to be dismayed and disgusted at myself. I must understand that to speak of any goodness of mine is presumption. I must confess that to expect salvation for anything that I have done is audacity. The younger son must long for the clean tranquillity of the old homestead, and forgiveness at the door.

Are you that son? The guilty girl, if the love of pure womanhood is not quite dead, must long for her Saviour's pardon and blessing. Are you the guilty woman,—guilty in imagination if not in act, in vanity if not in passion? You "professors of religion," you formal partakers at the altar, you may come regularly to church, but you will not find God here, or strength or light, unless you have done with the broken cisterns, the false interpreters, and your own self-will.

"Lord of the darkness and the day,
To Thee thy waiting people pray.
Perplexed, assaulted, hard beset,
Faithful we grasp thy promise yet.

"Dimly our homesick eyes descry
The signs that fleck earth's sunset sky;
But when we strive to read aright,
The evening deepens into night.

"Come, Prince of Life! Come, even so
As Thou from Olivet didst go;
Make good that word, for honor's sake,
The twain in white apparel spake.

"With cleansing fire, our work to try,
Discerner of the heart draw nigh,
Swing east, swing west, thy winnowing fan
Till judgment throughly search out man.

"So melts at last the twilight gray,
So broadens up the glorious day,
When stern to punish, swift to bless,
A King shall reign in righteousness."

TEACH us, O Lord, we beseech Thee, the way to Thee, the Shepherd of our souls, that turning away from all false and deceitful guides, and forsaking the broken cisterns which can hold no water, we may find in Thee that peace which the world cannot give or take away, and dwell with Thee evermore and world without end. *Amen.*

Fifth Friday.

WARNINGS OF JUDGMENT.

UNEQUIVOCALLY the Master speaks to us the words of warning. They are as much a part of His message to mankind as any words that He spoke. Whatever proportion they bear to different words, they have their fixed place. They are no more to be set aside, or passed over, or hidden, than any others. We may not be able wholly to explain them, but they are not to be explained away. "Wherever this Gospel is preached" warnings of judgment, of a real danger, of penalty for transgression, of a coming of the Son of Man which will bring with it terror to the disobedient, rejection to the unbelieving, and righteous retribution to the ungodly, must be heard. And because no mortal wisdom can supersede the Almighty authority, and no paraphrase represent the awfulness of inspiration, and no human assumption venture to add to God's Word or take from it, we can do no otherwise than to gather up and repeat them as they stand.

It was not in one of our man-built pulpits of wood or brass, but that mountain-pulpit which towers above all temples, and overlooks all continents and all centuries, that the Master Preacher said, in the compass of a sermon which covers but five pages, these sentences :—" Till Heaven and earth shall pass, one jot or one tittle shall in no wise pass from *the law* till all be fulfilled." " Except your righteousness shall exceed the righteousness of the Scribes and Pharisees, ye shall in no case enter into the Kingdom of Heaven." " Whosoever is angry with his brother without a cause shall be in danger of *the judgment*, and whosoever shall say to his brother, Thou fool, shall be in danger of hell-fire." " It is profitable for thee that one of thy members should perish, and not that thy whole body should be cast into hell." " Ye cannot serve God and Mammon." " Wide is the gate and broad is the way that leadeth to destruction, and many there be which go in thereat. Narrow is the way which leadeth unto life, and few there be that find it." " Every tree that bringeth not forth good fruit is hewn down and cast into the fire." " In that day I will profess unto—many —I never knew you ; depart from Me, ye that work iniquity." " Every one that heareth these sayings of Mine and doeth them not shall be likened unto a foolish man which built his house upon the sand; and the rain descended, and the floods came, and the winds blew, and beat upon that house, and it fell, and great was the fall of it." We may be preachers; we may be hearers; but one finds himself wondering whether this Preacher would be popular to-day. "When Jesus had ended these sayings, the people were astonished at His doctrine. For He taught them as one having authority." No ingenuity or exegesis can empty His language of alarm.

It may be that you do not like this. Between the ruler and the subject, between the master and his pupil, between a father and his child, between the law and those whom the law governs, there is sure to come a time when the subject, the pupil, the child, those who are governed, do not like what the ruler, the master, the father, the law, command. This question as to what we like can never be the first question in any society or condition of men, any people, or school, or family, or government in the world. Everywhere, somehow, the question of authority comes first; the right to command, the duty to obey. By some means or other this has to be settled, by strength, by wisdom, by age, by compact, by hereditary transmission. Every social and civil community on earth rests its welfare on this twofold and reciprocal principle, the right to command and the duty to obey, on authority. We here, all and every one of us, are in this relation to God, the Almighty, whether we like it or not, whether we will or not, whether we would be glad to have it otherwise or not. Here I assume that you acknowledge God to be Almighty, all-wise, all-good. You own that He is the Ruler, Father, Law-Maker of you and all mankind. By *every* right, by strength, by wisdom, by goodness, by His eternity, by our covenant with Him, by creating us, by keeping us alive, by infinite love, He has a right to command; our business is to obey. This building never would have been put up, the Bible would have been thrown away ages ago, worship would be nothing but a hypocrisy or superstition, the Prayer-book never could have been made, the pulpit would be an insufferable presumption, but for the settled fact that God's will is absolute, that His word *declares* His will, and that what He promises will be done. If, therefore, you say that you do not "like it," when He says, "Except ye repent ye shall all perish," when He says, "He that believeth shall be saved and he that believeth not shall be damned," when He says of unrepenting and unbelieving sinners, "These shall go away into everlasting punishment," you only say that you do not like God, do not like His Son your Saviour, do not like the government under which you live and will die. But that does not change Him, or remove the fact that what He has declared will be done.

To say nothing of the fearful maledictions and woes of many other passages, and nothing of the fearful explicit disclosures of judgment in the twenty-third and twenty-fourth chapters of St. Matthew, ponder the parables. Of the thirty no less than thirteen turn directly on the reiterated fact of a future retribution. See the tares and the burning of them; the draw-net and the bad fish cast away; the fruitless branches of the vine in the fire; the unprofitable servant doomed to outer darkness; the wicked husbandman destroyed; the ten virgins too late shut out; the utter rejection and misery inflicted for lack of the wedding garment; the unused talent a *damnum;* the barren fig-tree blasted; the rich fool and his shrivelled soul; Dives in torment; the Pharisee bidden to look straight at the damnation of hell. What can a reader of the New Testament, who reads in his right mind, mean by saying that Christ does not seek to save men by fore-warning them of the terrific consequences of their sins "pulling them out of the" metaphorical "fire"?

And this is the real and most gracious explanation of all that seems so hard. It is all to save. It is a Saviour's word and a Saviour's way. If you will let Him take His other and heavenly way, be sure He will gladly leave this way untrodden. No true father scourges his son but to receive him, and for the son's sake. It is love's altered voice, the merciful stroke of love's hand, delivered with anguish and pity unspeakable, infinitely reluctant, infinitely sad. Doubtless when our dear and loving Lord spoke those awful sentences there was a tenderness as of tears, a pathos unearthly in look and accent, such as you and I cannot imagine. Nevertheless there is a Throne, there is a Judge, there is a Right Hand and a Left. We cannot express it all so well as in the language which was spoken down from on high by Jehovah to His servant Moses standing on the mount with the two Tables in his hand: "The Lord descended in the cloud, and stood with him there, and proclaimed, The Lord God, merciful and gracious, long-suffering and abundant in goodness and truth, keeping mercy for thousands, forgiving iniquity and transgression and sin, and that will by no means clear the guilty."

You object to the threat of perdition as speaking to an inferior part of your nature. But nobody asks you, or bids you, or wants you, to repent, or to believe, or to be a Christian, or to live a holy life, from that inferior motive at all. Neither God nor His minister, neither the Bible nor the Church, wants you to be saved by terror of any punishment, or the dread of any pain. What *do* they want? They want to save you. They want you, yes, and they tell you, first and loudest, by every kindling promise and every inspiring prospect, to repent of sin because sin is foul and hateful in itself, degrading to manhood and womanhood, and insulting to God; to believe in God because He is your Father, and in Christ because He is your best and truest Friend, and in the Holy Spirit because He will quicken and comfort you. They bid you believe in another world because life there is bright and beautiful, perfect in charity, untroubled, spotless in purity, and noble; to believe in the Bible because it is your Father's message, the most wonderful of books, the flower and glory of the history and literature of men; and to believe in whatever is best and loveliest in humanity too, because humanity is God's child. Do you call *these* appeals to self-interest, or voices of alarm, or threats of penalty? But what then about those lower motives? Why, He who knows you better than you know yourself, and loves you better than you love yourself, cries to you with warning in the darkness, because you would not be led by His light. Whose fault is that? He went down to the lower part of you because you lived there, and cared for nothing above it. He shook you in your sleep, and roused you in your danger, with His merciful Hand, because you would not lean upon it and be guided and protected by it. He holds up His rod because you would not cling to His cross. By all means and by every means He will save you if you will consent to be saved.

"Searcher of hearts! Thou dost our ills
Discern, and all our weakness know;
Again to Thee with tears we turn;
Again to us Thy mercy show.

"Much have we sinned; but we confess
Our guilt, and all our faults deplore;
Oh, for the praise of Thy great name,
Our fainting souls to health restore!

"And grant us, while by fasts we strive
This mortal body to control,
To fast from all the food of sin,
And so to purify the soul."

O LORD JESUS CHRIST, who art coming again at the end of the world to judge the quick and the dead, have pity upon us in our sins, and so temper Thy justice with mercy that we may not be cast out in that day, but, together with those who have served Thee faithfully in their generation, may be admitted into the Courts of Thy House, eternal in the Heavens, there with angels and the spirits of the just to praise Thee evermore, who livest with the Father and the Holy Ghost, world without end. *Amen.*

Fifth Saturday.

THE DIVINE THIRST.

THERE is an inward thirst that is conscious and a thirst that though unconsious is not the less actual and significant. There are souls that long for God without knowing what they long for; and there are souls that, because they have begun to know and love God, long for Him the more. In the outer man thirst is natural and involuntary, a felt want of a needy and dependent bodily life. In the inner man it is a felt want of a needy and dependent spiritual life. One of the most striking of all expressions of it comes from a man who had found out by an extraordinary experience what is just as true of persons less extraordinary, when the two wants,—the inner and the outer—join their cries together: ' My soul is athirst for God; my heart and my flesh crieth out for the living God."

Think who it was that made this confession. The

greatest king of a great nation, so magnificent in his royalty that he was made a type of the Almighty King to come, to whom all the kingdoms of the earth belong. He was the greatest poet, too, of a poetical people,—singing such hymns to his harp that the whole Church of God, for nearly three thousand years, down to this very day, has kept on repeating them as the ceaseless and inexhaustible liturgy of its worship, because all its great ranks of intellects could make nothing like them. Such a man as this, a soldier, a monarch and a minstrel without a peer, having the Empires of military conquest, political power and literary fame at his feet, feels himself weak and empty and thirsty before God. Granaries filled with the finest of the wheat of fertile Palestine do not fill his hunger. The kingly power does not make him strong. The matchless music does not give him peace. The fountains of Mount Moriah and all the wines of the eastern vineyards do not slake a whit this *other thirst.* He knows what both thirsts are. Following the sheep as a shepherd-boy over Jesse's pastures he often got beyond the streams, and then he learned to say, "As the hart panteth after the water-brooks, so longeth my soul after Thee." In his wars and marches, hunted by Saul and the Philistines, fleeing from one mountain-cave to another, he panted like the deer he chased. Nothing in all the romance of any literature is more beautiful than the graceful adventure of the young heroes who followed him, breaking through the enemy's lines to get water for him, their leader, and then his pouring it out on the ground, as the costliest sacrifice he could offer, a gift of gratitude to Jehovah, and yet these sufferings only furnished him the agony to describe the keener longings of a penitent heart.

For, take notice, whatever the terrible agonies that David went through may have finally *made* him, in the purifying of his spirit, till at last he came to be called "a man after God's own heart," he certainly, in all that brilliant career where we behold him in his biography, was not at all what we understand by a saint. It is just there that a very common mistake is made. It was not because he was far exalted above the ordinary mass of men, in holiness or talent or station, but exactly the contrary, because he was a sinner like ourselves, was tempted and yielded to temptation, was ashamed of his iniquity, humiliated by his infirmity, tormented and terrified by his conscience, that he thirsted. It was because he remembered transgressions and crimes in his guilty days, such as none of us have committed. It was because he had found out that all his self-confidence was but a moving cloud, and his childhood's innocence like the early dew before a parching sun. It was because remorse had burnt it into him that he could do nothing, except blunder and fall, if he was left to himself. Judging by the fifty-first psalm, there has been no repentance on earth more thorough-going than his. On that ground he and we meet together. What he said we can say. What he felt, though his heart was under a royal robe, we can feel,—our mortal nothingness, our inability to cope with each day's dangers, our utter dependence on the grace of God. Helps we have that he had not. He was but the son of Jesse, the Bethlehemite, after all, and had never heard,—what every worshipper in Christ's Church has heard,—the divine story that afterwards began at that same Bethlehem and ended at the cross. He knew not the true Master and Redeemer, as we know Him. He only knew that he needed Him in his heart and in his flesh. Blessed are they that know that now!

How is it that *every* human soul cries out for God? Is there any true sense in which it may be said that men of every sort, good men and bad men and women, "professors of religion" and profane neglecters of its ordinances alike, thirst for the living God?

This much, at least, we all have in common. We have within us, as we may be sure, one human heart. Our Maker has put into every one of us a want of Himself. As He comes towards us in the living Person of His Son, there are voices of His own living Spirit within us, whether we heed them or not, pleading for Him. There are in every part of our being, secret thirstings and hungerings which nothing in the world short of Christ Himself, made our friend by faith, can satisfy. We may be too blind to see or too careless to consider what they mean. But this is what they mean. "Come unto Me, ye that labor and are heavy-laden, and I will give you rest:" "Whosoever drinketh of the water that I shall give him shall never thirst again:" "He that believeth in Me shall never die." Nothing less than this is the signification of these divinely kindled desires for the living God. We can take no credit for them. Our Father, in the great love wherewith He loved us before we loved Him, planted them in us, to draw us towards Christ, starting us in the road that leads to honor and glory and immortality. If we despise them, they will appear among our accusers in the judgment.

We need not travel far out of ourselves to hunt up arguments for the truth of our religion. Were we clearly conscious, as by prayer and faith we might be, of what we are, and what is going on within us, we should want no artificial evidences of the reality of the Gospel. God has written one Scripture and put it into our hands, to be our Book of Life. In the midst of its older Testament stands this: "My soul thirsteth for the living God." That is the prophecy. In the midst of His mediatorial ministry Jesus sits weary by the well, saying, "Whosoever shall drink of the water that I shall give him shall never thirst." That is the fulfilment. At the close of the Revelation of St. John, the curtains being lifted before the long succession of sinning and fainting souls to come, travelling homesick toward the great hereafter, the last apostle exclaims, "He showed me a pure river of water of life, clear as crystal, proceeding out of the throne of God and of the Lamb. Let him that is athirst come. And whosoever will let him take the water of life freely." That is the universal invitation. Another Scripture He has written in the spirit of man. Silently, but perpetually, it preaches to each of us its sermon for our salvation,—Come, and live. Some of you have not come. You think you have escaped the voice. But no! the voice is within you. It goes where you go, and you must hear it to the last. At Athens, when St. Paul preached on Mars Hill, in the centre of the learning and life of the eastern and western world, he said to the Greeks, "Whom therefore ye ignorantly worship, Him declare I unto you." Something like that is true for all unbelieving men.

"Low beside some fountain streaming
  I have knelt to drink,
There to quench my thirsty dreaming
  At its luring brink;
Thou didst trouble then the waters,
  Till I turned aside,
And I knew it was an angel
  Touched its failing tide.
Now the living fountain given
  Rises in its place,
And I rise from earth to heaven,
  Seeking, Lord, Thy face!"

O CHRIST JESUS, pour Thy grace upon us, we humbly entreat Thee; give us of the fulness of Thy grace; grant us love, purity, lowliness and patience; satisfy us with Thy mercy; and make us so truly to love Thee and without all doubt or deceit to glory in Thee, that we may draw perfect joy and peace from Thee alone, who livest with the Father and the Holy Ghost, world without end. *Amen.*

Fifth Monday.

MOUNTAIN AND MULTITUDE.

THE Master "seeing the multitudes went up into a mountain." And "He came down from the mount." He did that again and again. It forms a striking feature of His life. It must have been a necessity of His ministry and His Mediation. Society and solitude are conditions of a complete experience. In those three years of divine-human work which started the history of our race from a new beginning, and changed both the face and the heart of the world, there was nothing accidental.

Without doubt, in the change from publicity to retirement, and again from inaction to labor, our Lord found a personal refreshment. Such alternation between contact with people and a silent seclusion seems to come under a law that runs through body, mind and spirit. With most of us the continual presence and pressure of neighbors, the social strain, jostle and chatter, become at last tiresome and exhausting. There is a sense of waste. On the other hand, the same persons in prolonged and monotonous loneliness grow morbid and miserable. The same man longs to be alone, and to see faces and hear voices. Our Lord was a man. In His thoroughly human sensibility, with our nerves, sympathies, moods, He too must come under the same law, needing rest after toil, and activity after repose.

But the meaning is deeper. His presence with men was something more than mortal work, and His retirement was more than mortal rest. To Him what did "the multitude" signify? An untiring, unrewarded ministration of those gifts which He brought from the Father, a service of self-forgetful charity, a steady, sad accomplishment of the end for which He left the heavenly glory. What sore, straitening work it was! Sowing precious seed on stony ground; miracles of mercy that roused only a selfish and stupid gratitude; homeless travels; gracious helps held out which nobody accepted, and promises made which nobody understood; timid followers turning back; enmities provoked by unutterable tenderness; abuse, scorn, rejection, accusations of blasphemy! So He wrought all the day for "the multitude." He carried all this work up with Him in His heart to the "mountain." There alone He was to draw down out of the healing silence and infinite spaces, by direct communion with the heart of His Father, renewed supplies, wisdom for the teaching, power for the miracle, courage for the rebuke, patience for the pain. So He watched and waited in the still midnight. From thence, in the morning, from those high places of spiritual vision, elevations of the soul figured to our minds by hill-tops far above the fume and fret of men's frictions and disputings, by heights of land where the shadows of deep woods are blended with the mystery of sky and stars,—He was to bring fulfilments of the prophecy which had sounded along the same heights, "Peace on earth, good will to men." Such were the incomings and outgoings of His wondrous, redeeming life, the ascending of His prayers and the descending of His grace, the worship in the mount and the service in market-places and highways, a divine will and human hands, each helping the other, and both working out together new heavens and a new earth.

This habit of the Master, or rather the message proceeding from it, in its practical operation is larger yet. What was a fact in His personal life becomes a guide in the life of the whole Church, and in the life of every individual Christian. Because our Christian duty has just these two aspects. Regarded as a living force within us "the faith of the Gospel" is a treasure received by the faith of the heart, and it is a power of service to be put forth. A river of the water of life looks up to the spring it flows from and on to the fields it fertilizes. Mountain and multitude have a mutual relation, and exercise a reciprocal ministry. There is an altar-and-closet religion and there is an out-of-door religion; but these two are one. An unfruitful asceticism on one side and a prayerless philanthropy on the other would pull them apart. Those holy journeys of weary feet to the hills were no fanatic pilgrimages in spiked shoes to shrines of superstition. Those solitary hours were no retreat for barren reverie. They were as practical, in the larger and deeper view of what is practical, as the touch of the Lord's hand on the palsied and fevered sufferers in the city street or the washing of poor men's feet. Who knows that the blind would have been made to see, the lame to walk, publicans and sinners lifted out of their degradation, the Beatitudes proclaimed, the dead raised, but for those nights of prayer? In the Son of Man sanctuary and workshop are made to open into one another;

and in each He is equally at home and equally approachable. Not more perfectly harmonized are the Godward and manward look of the one Gospel of Love in the double commandment which is the evangelizing of the whole law than in the passing to and fro of the Mediator between the multitude of men and the mount of God.

"For thirty years to work with human hands
While love divine was yearning to express
The Infinite God's Heart which, grieving, longed
All weakness, sin and sorrow to redress!

Those patient, holy hands which humbly toiled,
Made lowly work for evermore confess
Work's innate worth, and, while He hallowed it,
He raised it to the height of nobleness."

"'Tis well to watch, all through these lonely hours
In the sad garden and beneath the cross;
'Tis well to give up something for our Lord
Who gave up all and counted life a loss.

"Yet, we may fill these quiet weeks of prayer
With sweetest charities for other's need;
With deeds and words of earnest Christlike love
Then shall we do God's work in very deed.

"With gentle home-work, doing all for love,
Making some life the better for our own;
Smoothing some path for other feet to tread,
Cheering some heart that has to work alone.

"So shall we live the nearer to our Lord,
So shall we labor through these Lenten hours:
Till Easter suns shall hail the golden day,
And joyful hands shall wreath the Easter flowers."

O MOST merciful Master, Christ, who hast bidden us to enter into the closet that we may seek Thee and find Thee in the secret place, and who hast commanded us to work while the day lasts in the field of Thy vineyard, grant, we beseech Thee, that we may follow Thee obediently, both in prayer and labor, that we may be strengthened with might from the mountain of Thy holiness and directed in all our service to our fellow-men, the children of Thy Father and our Father, unto whom, with Thee and the Holy Ghost, we render all honor and praise, world without end. *Amen.*

Fifth Tuesday.

WHAT IS REST?

THE call "come" has been sounded out over the earth in the ears of fifty generations of laboring, heavy-laden, restless men and women; and yet so many are tired, heavy-laden and restless still, it would seem that there must be some misunderstanding of the message. May it not be that a mistake attaches to the motive presented for the coming? To those who will choose Him, trust Him, and follow Him, Christ promises rest. If only a dreamy, soothing sentiment of repose steals over us as we read that promise, it will not move, it will not satisfy, it will not save the world. Indolent as many of us are, and weary as all of us sometimes are, there is something in us, after all, that makes us ashamed of easy aims. Even ordinary minds will turn away disgusted from a Gospel that offers them nothing but indulgence. To souls in earnest there comes a time, sooner or later, when they know that they ought to be uneasy, when they long for inward power, for purity, for righteousness, more than for comfort. In such loftier moments we say, "Give us a truth that will rouse us and yield us strength for work; do not talk to us of a Mahometan's heaven of idleness; we want a Gospel that will stir our energies, and inspire our lives to action, even if it costs hardship and causes us to carry a cross." Our Lord meets this better longing in many ways. He gives a new, original, and profounder meaning to this word "rest."

Three companies might be formed, no doubt, in almost any religious assembly of those who have not struck definitely into the way and work of the Christian life, coming for it to Him in whom it originates and of whom alone it can ever be had.

First are those who are satisfied, for the present, or imagine they are, with a kind of life which is in no honest sense the life of the Son of God; *i. e.*, His spirit of self-denying charity does not inspire and animate them; His command does not control them; and they hold no trustful or loving communications with Him. So far the great spiritual realities,—a personal God, the law of righteousness, the glorious beauty of holiness in the character of Christ, sin, judgment, the need to be forgiven,—have not smitten or shaken them, or broken the bright but unsubstantial dream which makes the world of the senses sufficient. We may not look at this pathetic spectacle, a heart lost without knowing it is lost, a gay surface and close below it terrible sufferings with such unutterable sadness and sympathy as the Saviour does, because we have neither His infinite love nor His penetratiug eyes to see all through and through the misery that is gathering and storing up; but none of us would think of applying to a life so shallow or so frivolous the word "rest," however merry or prosperous it might be.

Next are those who do not pretend to be satisfied, far enough from it, but have not yet done making experiments at it of their own, the same that have been going on ever since the self-will of the first man and woman broke away from God in Eden, in pleasure or pride, sensual prodigality, social prodigality, intellectual prodigality, of which the other names are dissipation, extravagance and unbelief. Conscience is not dead, but slowly dying, its disorder causing fearful pains before it finally expires. These are not brave enough or believing enough to arise and come, repenting and thankful, to the Giver of life; and certainly they are not "at rest."

The third, a company much larger than it ought to be after our eighteen centuries of heavenly grace on the earth, is made up of the victims of religious discontent. There is misunderstanding because there has been misinstruction. Nothing is clear. They thought they were going to be happy, but their bodies ache, and their hearts ache, like other people's; they are afraid to die; they have doubts; they are puzzled by the problems of Providence; they are not sure about answers to their prayers. Certain religionists tell them they must *feel* a great deal, but give them nothing to do, while the world with a much shrewder policy gives them a plenty to do, and then feeling takes care of itself. If they are Christians at all they are Christians of a complaining, half-hearted and second-rate sort, not much like those staunch disciples, of tranquil faith and joyful self-forgetfulness whose portraits are painted on the Scripture pages.

To these three restless ranks the Master patiently renews His great invitation, as long as the day lasts. And now here again in these Forty Days He is saying, "Come to Me,"—there is only one rest,—ye that labor with your hands, your brain or your heart; "I will give you rest."

What is it that He offers? Observe He is not

speaking of the next world, but of life here. What will He give now, at once, and all along? A very common idea of rest is that it is to stop work, to cease from effort, and do nothing. Is this the grand proposal from Heaven for man? How could He, the mightiest workman that ever touched the earth, the everlasting Laborer, promise *that* sort of rest to His people?

We are not so to understand Him. Looking deeper into all hearts and lives than we do He saw that most of our unhappiness springs from one of two sources; either that some duty is demanded of us which is not done, or else that burdens are put upon us which we are not willing to bear. On these two sore spots come the strain and the sorrow, the worst wear and tear, every day. Both the active and passive parts of our nature, the active by "labor" and the passive by being "heavy-laden," are overtasked. We suffer by what we have to do, and we suffer by what we have to endure.

The longer we think about it the plainer this will be. It is the inequality between what we are and what is required of us, or what we have and what we want, that is the secret of our restlessness and the tragic element in human life. We do not overtake what we are running after, and are weary. Our shoulders are not as broad and hard as the cross laid on, and we are heavy laden. Hence, from Adam going out of the gate of the natural Paradise to the Second Adam and His new creation, and from our own first cry in our mother's arms to the last convulsion, in all the chambers and the streets, the churches and the markets, the banquets and the battle-fields, humanity cries, O, make me equal to my needs; take away the disproportion, call it weakness or call it sin! Whoever will do that will be a Saviour.

Go out into the thoroughfares of the busy town and ask the men you meet what tires them. In the particular form of words the answers may be as many as the men, but under them all is one and the same sense. The man and the task are not equal. Necessity demands more, the passion for property thirsts for more, ambition aspires to more, the family ask for more, employers exact more than ability or time or skill can accomplish. If all were balanced, business and toil would be like play. The child at his lesson, the mother of the household, the banker, the politician, the preacher, the seamstress, look and sigh and wish they had more strength. Muscles and nerves are worn by friction and fatigue at night and are not always rested in the morning.

And so in the midst of them all, in the "noon and heat of the day," in shops, in fields, in high and lowly houses, at the entry of the city, at fashionable watering-places, by the wells of human learning, by pools of human blood, by voiceless graves, and at every heart's door, our Master Christ meets us and offers rest to all that will take it,—"whosoever will." As of old, some believe and some believe not. We will see to-morrow more of the pain, and more of the peace.

"My hands are weary, toiling on,
Day after day, for perishable meat;
O city of our God! I fain would rest,—
I sigh to gain thy glorious mercy-seat,

"My eyes are weary looking at the sin,
Impiety, and scorn upon the earth;
O city of our God! within thy walls
All, all are clothed again with thy new birth.

"My heart is weary of its own deep sin,—
Sinning, repenting, sinning still again;
When shall my soul Thy glorious presence feel,
And find, dear Saviour, it is free from stain?

"Patience, poor soul! the Saviour's feet were worn;
The Saviour's heart and hands are weary too;
His garments stained, and travel-worn, and old;
His vision blinded with a pitying dew.

"Love thou the path of sorrows that He trod;
Toil on, and wait in patience for thy rest;
O city of our God! we soon shall see
Thy glorious walls,—home of the loved and blest.

BLESSED Lord, who through all the days and nights of Thy years of mediatorial toil on the earth didst labor without wearying and didst possess Thy soul in perfect peace, give to us, Thy unprofitable servants, of Thy constancy in service and Thy patience in pain, while yet we remain here on the earth, and at length that perfect rest which remaineth for the people of God in His presence who liveth everlastingly, and world without end. *Amen.*

Sixth Wednesday.

NOBLE REST.

The Giver of life and strength being also the Giver of rest, it remains to see how this gift of rest is bestowed. When a load and the strength of its carrier are unequal there are two ways of equalizing them. You may take away a part of the load, or you may add to the carrier's strength. Either will accomplish the end. When a task is too much for a laborer you may bring the two together either by diminishing the task or by increasing the laborer's power. In relieving the workman the result in the two cases is the same. But as respects the amount of work done for the Master, and the honor of the workman, the results are very far from being the same. In the one case you rest the man by letting the work down to his infirmity, making it little for his littleness. In the other case you rest him and empower him together, by lifting him up to his high calling, inspiring and so comforting him.

If you look accurately at the matter you find that even in our earthly rests, a night's rest, or a vacation's rest, it is not a mere stopping from work that we gain, but far more than that, an increase of capacity and a replenishing of resources for service afterwards.

Now, to give His rest to our souls Christ never takes the first but always the second and more glorious of these two methods of relief. An accusing conscience being the burden, He never relieves it by dulling the sensibility of the conscience, or by merely striking out or cancelling the sin, as you would take out weights from the heavier side of an uneven balance. This is not the spiritual account of the atonement, but a belittling travesty of it. He rather stimulates and quickens that keen conscience in His disciple more and more; but then He supplies to the penitent believer such a living and holy power that all the sorrow and pain and fear are lost in this new energy and assurance from his Lord. He invigorates us with His inspiration. He fortifies us with confirmation-grace. He feeds us with sacraments. He revives us with answers to prayer.

So of the Christian's work. It is not shortened down to his mere natural ability. He is raised up and enlarged to the measure of its greatness. The Christian man is not told that he may do less service than the man of the world in order that he may be satisfied with himself. He has far more to do, more for man, more for God; but the Master he serves and in whom he believes furnishes him secretly, inwardly, spiritually, with a peculiar and glorious energy. He triumphs by his King.

The principle holds of all the sufferings and trials of Christian people. They are not exempt from the common liability to pain, or the necessity of discipline. They live in perishable bodies, among the same companions and in the same disordered world as irreligious men. Their nerves are as sensitive, their feelings as tender, their tastes as fastidious as other men's. The difference is that the sacrifices encountered are no more evils to them because they are met with another power of endurance, which is the mighty power of Christ in their hearts. God's will is their will. Thorns and thistles are turned into plants of heavenly nourishment for them. Paradise has been re-entered through Gethsemane. As the fall brought sweat and curse, because the inward man was crippled, the cross brings rest and blessing because by it righteousness becomes the choice and glory and joy of life, and He who suffered for us once dwells Himself, a conquering and peace-giving presence, in the new-born soul.

Doubtless, there might have been a different way. We can imagine a God working miracles to excuse His favorites from weariness of the flesh and anxieties of the mind, providing Arcadian inclosures where they could lounge away the idle hours, feast without surfeiting, and never know the torture of a cross. But then He would be a Pagan god in a heathen heaven. Jesus said, "Take My yoke upon you; carry My cross every day. Go work in My vineyard." He has too much work needing to be done and too deep a love for the workman to indulge us in any ignoble ease. He expects His Church to lead the world in unselfish activity, a laboring, giving, patiently-enduring Body of Christ. And all the strength necessary for it He supplies if only the channels of a receptive faith are open.

See the practical effect. When I have a fiery temper to manage, a trying lot to take patiently, a tiresome acquaintance or provoking neighbor to live with, bad habits to break down, any dark sin to conquer, or more of the new man to put on—ought I to ask that some Omnipotent Hand outside of me would sweep the obstacles away and make my road to Heaven smooth? This would leave me not a whit greater, holier, more Christlike than I was before. No, what I ought to ask is courage and endurance equal to my task, and a holy principle mightier than the temptation. That would be to be "strengthened with might by His Spirit in the inner man."

We come by this way into the deep places of the Gospel and the soul. We have found out just what "Gospel grace" is. It is our Lord's lifting Christians up into clear light and spiritual power out of their natural infirmities, enabling them for all their difficult work for God in this world. It is not letting their standard down, or abridging the march, or excusing them from battles. It is imparting to them a new life, larger life, a redeemed life, wide and grand with the fulness of God. Confess, then, how those parsimonious Christians dishonor and misrepresent their calling who drag on with indolent dispositions, mean dimensions, grudging charities or dainty fancies. The "Father worketh hitherto," and Christ, our King, our Prophet, and our Priest, gives all His life away. We can rise to meet our enemy on royal terms. We can look hostility in the face, as the look of fearless eyes is said to subdue lions. We can do all things through Christ strengthening us. Out of weakness, exactly as the apostle says, we shall be made strong, and when weakest in ourselves strongest for God. The strongest of you are impotent till you are on the side of the Almighty. Your incomes are impoverishing you, unless you would rather be poor than do wrong. Rest is not inaction, but liberty; not idleness, but willing and joyous movement forward. Rest is the perfect harmony and fulness of all the energies and affections of the soul, acting together by Him who fills all with His peace.

And here, finally, we have splendid outlines of what the Christian life hereafter will be. "This is life eternal;" life is action. Heaven will indeed be "rest," but not the rest of doing nothing. It will be intense, ceaseless, glorious work for God, every faculty free, every energy in play, every condition harmonized, and every breath thanksgiving. There shall be no night there, because there will be no need of any other repose or recovery or recreation than simply to live in a climate like that, a climate created by the Face of the Lord, who is the Everlasting Light. Day and night "they serve Him." Limitation, weariness, failure, suffering, sin are ended.

The discords of our cross-purposing and jarring plans with too much self-seeking in them, our jangling tempers and noisy passions, will be still. A few more of these twilights fading down the walls of the outer heavens that we see, and then the darkest and weakest mind among us will be able to comprehend what is the breadth. and length, and depth, and height.

"Where'er the gentle heart
Finds courage from above;
Where'er the heart forsook
Warms with the breath of love;
Where faith bids fear depart
City of Rest! thou art.

"Thou art where'er the proud
In humbleness melts down;
Where self itself yields up;
Where martyrs win their crown;
Where faithful souls possess
Themselves in perfect peace.

"Where in life's common way
With cheerful feet we go;
Where in His steps we tread
Who trod the way of woe;
Where He is in the heart,
City of God! thou art.

"Not 'throned above the skies,
Nor golden walled afar;
But where Christ's two or three
In His name gathered are,
Be in the midst of them
God's own Jerusalem."

O FATHER most merciful, who knowest all our necessities and infirmities, our discouragements in serving Thee and the burdens on our hearts, bestow upon us such strengthening and comforting grace, we entreat Thee, as may support us in all dangers to our faith, and carry us through all temptations to complaining or despair, through Him who toiled and suffered for our sake, Jesus Christ, Thy Son, our Lord. *Amen.*

Sixth Thursday.

DESCENDING AND ASCENDING.

It is given us to believe that there is going on now and always a twofold movement of the Life of God, a movement first downward of God to us, and then, answering to that, created by that, a movement in mankind of its believing and receptive souls upward towards Him. It is understood well enough that these terms downward and upward, below and above, are terms of metaphor, drawn from the world of sense and used in all language by accommodation as a part of the imagery by which alone we could conceive or express the realities of the spiritual world, making luminous the whole process of Revelation. The movement downward is one of loving kindness, help and renewal, making man's life like the life of God. It is not like the wind that blows down or the streams that fall from the hills, unconscious. It is personal, alive, having in it heart, mind and will. It is the uncovered secret of the everlasting mystery. It is characteristic of Christianity as distinguished from all false religions. One would suppose all the world would gladly believe it and welcome the gift. So far as it is believed, the kingdom of Heaven comes on the earth.

It strengthens us in the faith to see grand demonstrations of the fact standing out in one historic period after another in the religious training of the race. These "Dispensations" are only so many connected and successive ways of divine working by which the Head of the one great family educates His sons and daughters for a life like His own. Each has much about it that is unlike the others, as we might expect; and yet underneath the differences they are all one, because one purpose runs through them, and one Hand guides them. The unity is in Him who comes, and comes, and comes again. Superficial minds puzzle themselves over the Scriptures because instead of seeing the marks of a moral and divine unity, and being satisfied with them, they turn a microscopic criticism, partly finical and partly conceited, on obvious but insignificant differences, inseparable from a written Bible and a literary method. Once recognize the evidence that from

Genesis to the Apocalypse there runs a ruling and sublime design to open the unseen world down into this world by the Son of Man, a design manifest in some places and obscure in others, and details become subordinate and difficulties insignificant. The critics stumble into a barren and irrelevant skepticism by looking for proofs of inspiration with grammars and dictionaries and chonological tables, instead of being awed by the simple and majestic fact, unmatched in all literature and history, that Providence has for a wonderful end brought and held these ancient writings together through the ages and for all nations, the Incarnation being the bond of their unity, the theme of patriarchs and prophets, psalmists and historians, evangelists and apostles.

The first age reaches from the first Adam to the second, from Eden to the birth at Bethlehem. Throughout are clear signals of the descending and ascending movement. Notice the order, not ascending first, as if everything originated with man, as if he made his own religion, sent his own Saviour, constructed his own Church, invented his own cross, and by a pull of several thousand years drew himself up into heavenly places; but descending first. The power originates not on the human but on the divine side; not, as the rationalist imagines, with those who being helpless need to be helped, and being lost need to be found, and born bad need to be born again, but with the Almighty Maker, Helper, and Finder. The entire sweep and meaning of the record strike squarely against the theory that man elevates, purifies, saves, or even civilizes himself. God moves first for the soul of His child. The child is moving not towards Him but from Him. The first line of Scripture signalizes the entire era, "In the beginning God." That keynote rings through the Old Testament voices till the last of its prophets announces the Word made flesh. Over all those Eastern plains, moving before the eyes of men, the Leader, Ruler, Pleader, Preacher, Deliverer, is one not of this world. He wants His straying, blinded, homeless children with Himself, out of the desert and miry clay, out of the dark, out of the prison-house, out of the far country of harlots and swine, heathenism and hatred, the shadow of death, and they must be lifted out. The eyes that are bent earthward must be turned Heavenward, and then heart and hope will be turned. They have not the power, the knowledge, the sight, not even the dream. And when there is a way disclosed, a Hebrew Church set up, a people redeemed, a worship in the wilderness, the cloudy pillar "descends, stands at the door of the Tabernacle, and all the people rise up."

This pillar is not God, or Christ, or the Holy Spirit. It is an external thing. God is not yet known or felt by men as within them, dwelling in their hearts, or even a Presence among them, walking at their side. Above them He certainly is, a glorious and worshipful Reality there. He comes to them from without, looks on them, speaks to them, directs them, pleads tenderly with them, never forgets them. Yet He is thought of and spoken of chiefly as elsewhere. At first there is not even a special outward seat of His glory. In the Patriarchal age the heavens enthrone and hide Him. Messengers come, and they always come down. They visit men at their doors, at midnight, in holy places, by ladders of light. The other world is open, but distant. The forms of its bright inhabitants gleam through shaded pathways. Supernatural manifestations are never incredible. Clouds are touched and mountains are crowned with their splendor. Nobody is greatly surprised by a celestial visitor or disputes his credentials. Whatever weakness, or sins, or crimes there may be, such as we have to witness and deplore now, there is none of our wretched, shallow, upstart materialism. Men and women live every day in the faith of a larger, higher and better world than this. The centre and throne is there—the seat of power, of light, of welfare. The earth is troubled and transient. Heaven is steadfast and eternal. Every movement of mercy is started there.

To make the invisible more definite, and to bring it within the easier grasp of all orders of minds, these heavenly realities are symbolized and thus localized. God's people are planted in one country. The Divine Majesty has an earthly court. There is a theocratic commonwealth, a holy nation, a constitution, a ritual, a tabernacle, a temple, a shekinah, a priesthood, a Moses in the mount and an Aaron at the altar. No one supposes these things originated on the earth, were a human product contrived in the brain of any man. The brain was less active than it is now, but it knew better than that. Men knew their needs, infirmities, dependence better, and they knew God better. The wisdom that ordered this visible worship, the foresight that planned both tabernacle and temple, the pardon in the sacrifices, the light within the light, came from beyond the flight of the eagle, the hiding-places of the thunder and the chambers of the sun-rising. All beginnings were seen to be in God. The unchanging residence of all peace and love, power and protection was on high. The downward and upward movement went on. "The cloudy pillar descended and stood at the door of the tabernacle." Prophets preached, priests ministered, Psalms were sung to David's harp, fire fell, incense arose, Israel was led and ruled, in the same faith. Jerusalem itself, the city of the Great King, was not the centre of life, the fountain of dominion, or the foundation of the throne. Patterns of holy things were let down from a loftier mount. All was done to lift men upward, and they were lifted. "The people rose up and worshipped." We are their children, their heirs. Is their faith our inheritance?

"As the deep blue of Heaven brightens into stars,
  So God's great love shines forth in promises,
Which, falling softly through our prison bars,
  Daze not our eyes, but with their soft light bless.
Ladders of light God sets against the skies,
Upon whose golden rungs we step by step arise,
Until we tread the halls of Paradise."

O ALMIGHTY God, who hast created the heavens and the earth, and who hast opened the heavens to the earth that men might behold Thy glory in the doing of Thy will, and be drawn upward to dwell with Thee in Thy unseen and everlasting habitation, grant, we beseech Thee, that as Thy holy angels always do Thee service in Heaven, so they may succour and defend us on earth, through Him who hath brought life and immortality to light, our Saviour, Jesus Christ. *Amen.*

Sixth Friday.

HEAVEN SHUT AND OPENED.

It sometimes seems that the Christian family, in spite of all its gains, along with some things that it could better spare has parted with a portion of its birthright. Allowing that some delusions have been dispelled, some idols broken, and some better interpretations of obscure Scriptures found out, we nevertheless rise sometimes from the reading of those "lively oracles," or from the writings of saints of an elder time, with a feeling that a glory not of the earth has passed away from it, because so generally men look to themselves rather than to God, around them rather than above them, to the works of their hands and the creatures of their imaginations rather than to Him who hangeth the earth upon nothing and "maketh His angels spirits"? If the Bible is the Book of man's life, can it be that the living multitudes which in all the Bible-times from first to last came and went in the paths and habitations of men, joined in their worship, witnessed to them of untrodden tracts of the universe, have swept by like shadows of the night or phantoms of its sleep? Is all that is above our heads a vacuum, a blank, an unreality? The school-house, the college, the chemical laboratory, the museum of natural history, the microscope, do a great deal for us; do they, have they ever, will they ever, create a conscience, forgive a penitent, quench lust, heal the broken in heart, publish a Gospel, redeem a soul? Would it damage our civilization if its leaders, or our industries if their masters, believed in beings that eye hath not seen or ingenuity contrived? Would it even hinder our speed or stop the spindles or spoil trade if all the while the people should commune with Heaven and take spiritual gifts from on high? Is there any reason why business-men should be less strong in their hands and feet because, before their business or after it, they are on their knees? I believe there could be no grander deliverance of the religious mind of this people into liberty and light and joy than by a restoration of the early faith in the constant nearness of the unseen world, by feeling inspirations in daily duty to come to us out of its heights, and by a living sense that our Lord in Himself,—He in us and we in Him—holds the common and the heavenly spheres in "one communion" together.

To this communion He constantly draws the minds of His followers. It is, therefore, not something speculative or unpractical. He points to His heavenly origin only that He may reveal the obligation and furnish the power to our living the heavenly life here. Joining God's life in Him with the human life in us He gives His disciples a knowledge that they too in a real sense "came forth from God." This new creation is in the individual and in His mystical Body, as if the Church had a kind of moral personality of its own. St. Paul taught it, how clearly! The first man is of the earth, earthy; the second man is the Lord from heaven. "As is the heavenly, such are they also than are heavenly."

Without that descending grace and glory, this mortal stir at its best and bravest, what would its life be? A "little life" indeed, and "rounded with a sleep." "Except a man be born again he cannot see the kingdom of God." One would suppose every son and daughter of man would welcome so large a truth, so substantial a gift and so inspiring a promise. So far as it is really and heartily believed, God's kingdom comes here on the earth.

Whatever other things you may call by the name of religion, in doctrine or practice or philosophy or ceremony, this righteousness beyond the righteousness of Scribe and Pharisee, the righteousness of "God over all" wrought into character in men, is the religion of Christ.

Yes; so is the coming of the kingdom. Who is wise to understand this thing? Who has lips to declare it? "Entering into life" is not having a passage way cut in the wall through which by-and-by our souls may creep into heaven to get their first acquaintance with it. There is present, immediate, open intercourse. We have our refreshments where we need them most, here, fighting temptation, serving our neighbors, forgiving enemies, returning good for evil, bearing pain. You will be better every way and everywhere, better scholars at school, better workmen, better guides, better nurses or patients, better husbands or wives, better employers or wage-workers, for faith in open heavens, in Him who "has ascended up on high giving gifts unto men."

With all its failures and disgusts, its sicknesses of heart and flesh, its emptiness and folly and the sin that is worse than either, to a believing resident in it "this present world" is an outer room at least of the great House of God. The Church itself is sacramental, under the outward sign of the visible body an indwelling and gracious and quickening power of life. Members of it whose membership is of the spirit and not of the letter only can say with angels and archangels, "Lord God of Hosts, Heaven and earth are full of Thy glory. Glory be to Thee, O Lord, Most High!"

Father divine! this deadening power control,
Which to the senses binds the immortal soul;
O, break this bondage, Lord, I would be free,
And in my soul would find my heaven in Thee.

"My heaven in Thee! O God, no other heaven
To the immortal soul can e'er be given:
O let Thy kingdom now within me come,
And as above, so here, Thy will be done!

"My heaven in Thee, O Father, let me find,
My heaven in Thee, within a heart resigned;
No more, of heaven and bliss, my soul, despair,
For where my God is found, my heaven is there."

O THOU who hast set Thy glory above the heavens, and yet hast condescended in Thy Son to make Thy dwelling with the sons of men, wilt thou graciously assist us by Thy Spirit, that coming down from on high in the majesty and tenderness of His heavenly power and love He may enter into our hearts in these days of our humiliation and abide there continually, that following Him in His suffering and triumph we may behold Him as He is and worship Him on the throne of His glory, world without end. *Amen.*

Sixth Saturday.

LAW MADE HONORABLE BY SACRIFICE.

THE Scriptures for this day sharpen the contrast between the old covenant and the new, the law of ordinances and the grace of the Gospel, Moses and Christ, at the same time that they show the connection between them in the one eternal plan of God for man. It all signifies also the spiritual advance from the old to the new creature. In the formation of Christian character the process may be sudden or gradual. But we come first to obedience as duty, on pain of a penalty. With this is inseparably connected repentence true or false. Each of the sensual iniquities has its own punishment in some natural disorder, a penalty in kind. Spiritual sins, like pride, insincerity, disbelief, irreverence, though their distressing consequences are more obscure, are equally sure to be overtaken sooner or later by their appropriate retributions. We are advertised beforehand of these inevitable consequences. Hence the commandments. They are written really in the Bible, the conscience, and the experience of life.

You can shut the first of these books, where they are most clearly written, if you please, because you find the subject disagreeable, and this accounts for the unopened Bibles lying in so many houses. But you cannot shut the other two ; and if you could, the retributive pain would still keep wasting and throbbing on, in your aching body or aching heart. If you stay in that comprehensive state of sin, where the whole nature stands estranged from God, and hides from Him, sometimes called impenitence and sometimes unbelief, then the retribution will be equally comprehensive and complete ; it is that final separation from God of which the issue is perdition.

In all this there is nothing very inspiring or refreshing. On the contrary, it is the very thing that creates penitential sorrow. When the commandment came, sin revived. It told you what wrong-doing was, and made you conscious of it. The more law you had, if it was nothing but law, the more you wanted some reconciling grace, because your nature was bad, and your transgression certain. You know that the law is necessary to keep the world in order, and that the world would go straight to wreck and ruin without it.

But to you personally it is simply a sentence of condemnation. It is a hard fact. It is a rock of offence in your way. You are constantly chafing against it. In the outward world around us law is beautiful and beneficent, in the seasons and harvests, in the sea and the stars; for then there is no element at war with it. But man is a moral creature and lives in a moral sphere. He has disease in him, bad desires and bad blood; and, therefore, unless there is some remedial force, some healing agency, some Saviour and Deliverer to work a change *within* him, reconciling and purifying him, why, God manifested only as law will be dreaded and avoided.

What then is the use of so much law? If God loves us, why does He not deal with us in some other way? Why must this Israel in every man's heart carry about, in the pilgrimage of life, this heavy burden in the breast, to try him and to prove him whether he will keep God's commandments or no?

The answer to these questions is the Gospel's dearest, deepest secret. We should never have known the delicious sweetness of God's forgiving love but for the violated law which made the forgiveness wonderful. The New Testament could never have been written, if the Old had not been written first. The Cross would have been only two transverse pieces of common wood, except for all those foregoing failures of the human conscience to "fulfil the law's demands." I hear God say, "The soul that sinneth it shall die." I know that sin is the transgression of the law. For the life of my soul I try to obey all that "commandment," which is so "exceeding broad." What then if I see the Son of Man lifted up, and hear Him say, "Only believe, and thou shalt live! Instead of the deeds of the law, thy faith saves thee. Go in peace! Be united to Me by that living bond of love and truth, and out of this heart of infinite love and purity and life in Me life eternal shall flow into that stained and fainting heart of thine. Because I live thou shalt live also"? Will not that be the good news from a far country, well water to a thirsty soul? Is it not the very Gospel that we have?

Among strong, upright and beautiful characters that we have known, none are so strong, so upright, and so beautiful as those where the graces grow on the firm stock of obedience. Goodness is never very good, tenderness is not nobly tender, unless there is conscience under it, principle in it. Fetch back the old Hebrew and Puritanic idea of allegiance and you restore some nobilities that we can ill afford to spare. Religion should not be an effeminate sentiment, or faith a headstrong fanaticism. The clamor for more "rights" is justified only when rights are wanted as affording means and opportunities for duty. Otherwise staunch manhood will be scarce, families will be little "fierce democracies," schools impertinent insurrections, government the cowed victim of anarchy, and the Church a congregation of volunteers divided against itself even while it is saying its prayers. The Lord Himself, Master of all kingdoms, was subject to parental rule, obeyed the barbarous "powers" of the empire, conformed to the ritual of the theocracy, and so laid His blessing on the foundations of the three enduring pillars that God has set to uphold the welfare of the world, the Family, the State, the Church.

"Three roots bear up Dominion,—knowledge, will,
These two are strong, but stronger yet the third,
Obedience, the great tap-root which still,
Knit round the rock of duty is not moved
Though war's fierce ploughshare spend its utmost skill."

In the great vision of St. John, the upper and inner heavens being disclosed, the seer saw a "rainbow round about the throne." A rainbow without the throne would have been a spectacle to be admired. A throne without the rainbow would have meant sovereignty without mercy, law without grace, a wild and stormy splendor without the promise and pledge of peace. "Justice and judgment" would be still its "foundation"; but who would sing the new song, the praise of the "Lamb slain"? As the blood is precious, so it is costly. We can draw towards the scene of the agony fearfully and only as "sheep that have gone astray"; but we "venture near" boldly because "on Him is laid the iniquity of us all."

"Angel of pain, I think thy face
Will be, in all the heavenly place,
The sweetest face that I shall see,
The swiftest face to smile on me.
All other angels faint and tire,—
Joy wearies and forsakes desire;
Hope falters, face to face with fate,
And dies because it cannot wait;
And love cuts short each loving day,
Because fond hearts cannot obey
That subtlest law which measures bliss
By what it is content to miss,—
But thou, oh loving, faithful pain!
Hated, reproached, rejected, slain,
Dost only closer cling and bless
In sweeter, stronger steadfastness.
Dear patient angel, to thine own

Thou comest, and art never known
Till late in some lone twilight place
The light of thy transfigured face
Sudden shines out, and speechless they
Know they have walked with Christ all day,"

O THOU who by Thy pain, borne for us, hast made pain to bring patience, and by Thy death for us hast overcome death, grant that following after Thee in the path of Thy obedience even to Thy Passion, where Thou wast obedient to the law for men, we may find it to be none other than the way of pardon for ourselves and victory and peace with Thee, who having died unto sin once livest and reignest with the Father and the Holy Ghost, now and evermore. *Amen.*

Monday in Holy Week.

ROCK AND WATER.

By the history of Israel, and by St. Paul's Epistle to the Corinthians, we have to-day at once the miracle of the bringing of water from the rock and the interpretation of that type in the spiritual gift provided in Christ for the Church. Three figures carry the mind beyond the bounds of natural fact. Men drink of a stone; the rock leaps out of its bed, joins a caravan and moves with it as if it had life; and then the rock is no more so much mineral matter, but the Son of Man, man's Saviour. We are so made that we have no great difficulty, but rather a luminous guide, in discovering what the great good News has to teach us by this threefold wonder of a stone-fountain giving life to an Eastern multitude journeying across a desert. "I would not have you ignorant, brethren, how that all our fathers were under the cloud, and all passed through the sea, and were all baptized into Moses in the cloud and in the sea, and did all eat the same spiritual meat, and did all drink the same spiritual drink; for they drank of that spiritual rock which followed them, and that Rock was Christ." Why are we taken back, at the opening of our Holy Week, through two long removes and periods of time, first to a Corinthian community buried eighteen centuries ago, and then to a strange people almost twice as remote, into a dim age and a vanished host, to learn the lesson of a universal law and an everlasting life?

Because in all generations and lands the human heart is one and the same thing, and every one of us has it in his own breast. It has to do with one and the same God and Father. It is weak and defiled with the same infirmities and sins. It can be strengthened only by the same power from on high. It feels the same mysterious forebodings of a judgment to come. It has the same conscience, love, fear, and, when it has put its lips to broken cisterns, the same returning thirst. No shifting of the course of empire, east or west, as the desert sands are blown by the winds, no building or burial of cities, can change the substantial nature and wants of the soul. This is the secret of that indestructible hold which one old Book, as fascinating in its charm as it is awful in authority, keeps and promises to keep on mankind. Superficial critics, dealing only with surfaces, dates, the letter, the shell, miss the meaning. "The letter killeth, the Spirit giveth life." Israel is man. Egypt is the broken condition of the moral life. Passions and appetites in our flesh and mind are Pharaoh. The wilderness is human experience. The forty years, patterns of these forty days, are the trial and the discipline. The pillars of cloud and flame are the unsleeping Providence. The baptism of cloud and sea is the baptism of water and the Holy Ghost. The manna is the bread of life in Him who is from Heaven, on whom except we feed we die. The land of promise is the end of our faith. This is why we hold so fast the story of what you may call, if you are shallow enough, the romance of a departed system and a scattered race. This is why all the Christian phraseology of the Church down to this year of grace is sprinkled with Jewish names and colored with Oriental allusions. That is why evangelist and apostle, and the Master Himself, scarcely speak of the permanent realities of the kingdom of Heaven without some name, or memorial or metaphor from that unforgotten pilgrimage of the tribes. You rise to loftier apprehensions of God's plans running through the dispensations and binding them together. You behold the magnificent unity which not only links the epochs of Revelation in one, but which also identifies your own personal struggles and sorrows and deliverances with those of the fathers fallen asleep. They did eat of your meat; you drink of their water of life, for "that Rock was Christ."

What more unlike than rock and water? No solvent can make a stream of a stone. It refuses to be assimilated to any vital organization as refreshment or nourishment. When Jehovah set a natural gateway to Palestine west of the Jordan, and made its mountain-posts, Ebal and Gerizim, monuments of warning and promise, He put the curses on dry Mt. Ebal, a rocky peak, ridged with sharp edges, leafless, blossomless, fruitless, waterless, symbol of a barren commonwealth and a faithless Church. Yet notice that under certain conditions, provided you take it for what it is and was meant to be, a rock with all its rigidity may become a kind of external protection, a shadow from the heat or a shelter from the storm. Hungry or thirsty, for all that it can do for you, you would die. But be friendly with it and you may lean upon it. It never betrays you or plays you false. It abides. It keeps its place.

Hence in some of His steadfast attributes the Almighty is often called in His word by this figurative name. The rock is not evil, cruel, malignant. Only when you ask it to be or do what it cannot do, it disappoints you.

Rock stands then significantly for the law. The spiritual world, like the material universe, has its stability and security in law. The framework of the globe is braced up by the firm pillars and buttresses of subterranean stone. God is the one Lawgiver. Could we only live on confiding terms of obedience and submission with it, we should find His orderly will to be our cradle and our castle. But no man ever found the slaking of his inward thirst, satisfaction of love, or hope, or aspiration, in commandments. When he cries out for affection, for pardon, for peace, he knows that mercy is not in rules. They are fitly written on tables of stone. Law is rock. The more of that you give him the more he aches and despairs. If the law could have given life you would have needed no Gospel, cross, Holy Week, redemption. When the soul longs after God as the hart panteth after the water-brooks, it is not His statutes that will cool or slake the thirst. The rock holds up the soil, the green turf, the trees, the harvests, the water-brooks themselves. But it gives life to nothing. It quiets no accusing conscience. It heals no troubled breast. Sinai, seat of thunderings and threatenings, was rocky. How vividly St. Paul represents it! "The ministration of death was written and engraven in stones." But we, planted in the New Jerusalem, "above and free," born again in a more lasting covenant, gathering around the cross, are not come to Mt. Sinai in Arabia which gendereth to bondage, but to a larger liberty and the "bringing in of a better hope."

That is, there is another and more gracious element, different in form, in substance, in effect. The kingdoms of vegetable and animal organization, of life and living things, are revived, invigorated, and made fruitful by water. Water is at once yielding, penetrating, and life-giving, and it fulfils its ministry not by remaining a mere outside minister, but by entering into hidden pores and vital channels, by becoming an internal force, and thence feeding all the springs of action. He who knew what it is, and what it does, and who knew from how much higher a source it flows than the fountains of Gerizim, and how much deeper it is than Jacob's Well in Samaria, called it "the water of life," a "well of water springing up into life everlasting."

Here is the graciousness of the gift. Grace is the freeness of love, unmerited, unhindered, impartial love. Law is behind it, regulating it, preparing for it, securing its channels. The water is from the rock. Love presses, melts and winds its way into our inner hearts. There it quickens all that is best, and purifies what is base, and sweetens what is bitter. Love is the fulfilling of the law. In these shaded hours, this tender worship, ashamed of the sins past, knowing that unless we are pardoned we perish, we adore Him who by His Cross magnified the law and made it honorable, yet fulfilled it by His love.

"They have stopped the sacred well which the Patriarchs dug of old,
Where they watered the patient flocks at noon, from the depth so pure and cold;
Where the Saviour asked for drink, and found at noon repose;
But the living spring He opened then no human hand can close.

"They have scattered the ancient stones, where at noon He sat to rest;
None ever shall rest by that well again, and think how His accents blessed;

But the Rest for the burdened heart, the Shade in the weary land,
The riven Rock, with its living streams, forever unmoved shall stand."

"They lead Thee forth to die,—
The Lamb, the sinless One;
In lonesome agony.
Thy Father's will is done:
But we believe Thy dying cry
Our life eternal won.

"While Thee, O Saviour dear!
We watch this holy week,
O teach us how to bear
Our cross with spirit meek;
And we believe Thy love is near
To grant the best we seek."

O THOU who by Thy gracious power bringest waters of life out of the hard rock, light out of darkness, good out of evil, and immortality out of the grave, grant, we beseech Thee, that by the sorrows of repentance our souls may be made glad, by suffering with Christ we may be glorified with Him, by days and weeks of mourning we may come to the joy of a blessed resurrection, and by our bearing patiently whatever afflictions Thou seest fit to lay upon us here Thy mercy may work out in us the peaceable fruits of righteousness, through Jesus Christ our Lord. *Amen.*

Tuesday in Holy Week.

PARTAKERS OF CHRIST'S SUFFERINGS.

THE one fact in the experience of men that stands before us now is suffering. Gathering us around the foot of the cross the Church shows it to us once more in its supreme majesty and its indescribable agony in the Son of Man. The days when those we love best die are never like other days. It is one of the signs of the mastery of the interior world over the outward world, the superiority of a human passion to all the great powers of nature in earth and sky, that the very look of common things about us, the light or shadow on the landscape, the feeling of the air and the sounds in the street, are mysteriously touched and changed by a stroke of anguish falling silently on the heart. The scene at Calvary would make no penetrating or profound impression if suffering were not a terrible reality in every one of our own lives. We realize the crucifixion in whatever measure we feel Christ to be a fellow-sufferer, crying aloud for pain, and yet pitying and forgiving His crucifiers.

The thought then to be taken into our minds, so that it may take root there and become a living and growing thought, is this: the connection between Christ's sufferings and our sufferings; the common element in His great cross and our little crosses, drawing us all closer to Him in the wonderfulness, the tenderness and the glory of His willing sacrifice, and bringing Him also nearer to ourselves in our own pain—that pain, of one sort or another, which somehow or somewhere, sooner or later, in flesh or nerves or brain or conscience or soul, in disease or accident, from ill-will or hatred or slander, by personal sorrow or sympathy with others, we have to bear, everyone, whether we will or not. Think what different things they must be for us to go through *with* Christ and *without* Christ. Strike them out of your life altogether, and you would empty the Scriptures we read this week of their meaning. The preaching of atonement and redemption would sound like a fiction. This holy time of the Passion would be like ordinary time. You might then pull down all the images of the cross from the churches, or throw them away from your breasts, and leave no blank, and feel no loss.

We worship the Divine Sufferer because we know what it is to suffer.

First in the common spiritual condition where we are, of which we know only that our Father has appointed it, it is a law that we can attain to the highest and noblest and best that is possible for us only through a pathway of pain. Like our Master and with Him we learn not only "obedience" but liberty, not only duty but blessedness, and not only strength as we go on but immortal victory at last, by some unwelcome discipline which is to us, for the time, a cross, something which takes that shape and has that sharpness. Except we take it up and carry it, following Him, we are not disciples or disciplined; a thing so easy to hear said in a sermon or to be read in a book, but so hard to receive when it comes to us in our life. The office for the Visitation of the sick in the Prayer Book, with solemn beauty says, "He went not up to joy but first He suffered pain; He entered not into His glory before He was crucified." Just as plainly does the writing written all along the way of our life say, that only as first we bear some distress we go up to any lofty height of character. The Bible in our hands and the Bible of God's revelation in the history of man agree.

Does this perplex our understanding? It is possible for us so to interpret the law, and so to conform our heart and will to it, that it shall cease to be forbidding, or disheartening, or embittering, or a stumbling-block of contradiction or unbelief, and become instead a means of thoughtful satisfaction. A faculty is furnished you in your very nature, and it will wake up and open and drink in light, if only you will let it, by which your dismay will be turned into peace, and your terror into a triumph. "Think it not strange concerning the fiery trial which is to try you, as though some strange thing happened unto you; but rejoice inasmuch as ye are partakers of Christ's sufferings." No human tongue could say that, which had not learned it from a hidden teacher in the soul. I doubt whether any of you, merely hearing the words repeated, take the truth in or recognize it as anything more than a pious fancy, unless there has been some inward taste and proof of its reality. How was it? The shadow of death fell on a countenance in your house which was to you like the light of the morning, changed it, and it had to be sent away and buried under ground. A presence which never did you anything but good all the days of your companionship vanished. A child or brother that you had built up strong castles for in your dreams, and asked of God all blessed things for in your prayers wanders into the far country, lost. Some hope that had lightened the hardships of poverty or solitude for years is broken to pieces at your feet. Or the memory of an old sin or shame hangs a sullen cloud over every scene where others make merry and are glad. You look at the happier lot of a man or woman who grew up at your side, you mark the contrast, you think of what might have been, you put out your hand and there is no support, and you say, "This is a 'strange thing' that has 'happened' to me. It is a strange world to live in. It must be a strange God that governs it"; no satisfaction, no triumph, no peace there. But a man who once went out from the face of his Lord and wept says, "Think it *not* strange concerning the fiery trial." It *is* "fiery," there is no denying that. I know and you know how it burns, scorches, turns beauty to ashes; but the strangeness is not the strangeness of accident, or caprice, or mockery, or carelessness. It has not "happened" to you at all. Love that is infinite never mocks, never tantalizes, never forgets. Did you ever do that with your mother or your child? and your love is not infinite. "If ye then being evil know how to give good gifts unto your children, how much more shall your heavenly Father," yes, even when the good things come wearing the aspect and the name of losses, or bereavements, or disappointments! Providence never blunders. He who keeps the stars punctual and the wheels of the universe running in order, who without slumbering watches the sleep of all His fourteen hundred million children every night, makes no mistakes; He is never taken unawares by a disease or a cloud. The mystery *is* a mystery, but it has a revelation within it, and it brings heavenly gifts under its wings. What did your Maker put the faculty of faith into you for, when He gave you a body and made it tender, and gave you feeling and reason and memory and hope? Why was His perfect and spotless Son poor, homeless, disappointed, rejected, buffeted? Why, as on this week, did He die as robbers and murderers die, when He might have lived on earth as kings live, or swept Pilate and Herod and Judas and the Sanhedrim and the Roman Empire off the earth together by twelve legions of angels? Call it a mystery if you please; these are the mysterious facts that are the honors of history and the glory of the world. You can do better. You can rise, and climb, and be tranquil, and say, "Thy will be done," and look on the world around you with sweeter charity, and look down with gentler comparison on feebleness, and look up with a surer confidence and expectation into heaven, and be strong. "Think it *not* strange." "Rejoice, inasmuch as ye are partakers of Christ's sufferings," for this was *His* rejoicing. "If we suffer with Him, that we may be also glorified together."

A few uncommon spirits find their way into the everlasting peace without the spur or scourge of grief. But so rare is this, even in this Christian age and country, where the Gospel Feast is spread everywhere, that when we see grown men and women coming in from the world to the Church the question rises, "What *sorrow was it* that roused at last and wakened this soul to life? Was it sickness, was it a business failure, was it a broken family circle, a broken heart, a broken wedding-ring?" At any rate there was the pang of a contrite conscience. Be not afraid of that! And so when we see a household yet unreached and unrenewed by the Spirit of Truth, a man living only for what is outside of him, a woman who has taken flattery for her guide and admiration for her comforter and pleasure for principle, with a giddy head, a frivolous heart and an unchastened temper, then a sober experience asks, What will the trouble be which is to shake this loose fabric of treacherous confidence to pieces, blight this beauty, scatter this wealth, disturb this dream? Which friend will betray? Which bubble of speculation will burst? Which sin will find the sinner out and drag him to the judgment? He who knoweth every frame, O thoughtless and unbelieving child, will suit the medicine to the disorder. Why wait till you are hurt, bleeding, humiliated, starved, or eating with swine, every kind of "substance" wasted, before you arise and come home?

On the other hand, if you will read a brighter testimony of the wonder-working transformation of the cross, study the marvellous process by which your Master changes the things that we dread, and run away from, into helpers and ministers of grace. To-day, in your neighborhood, you go into a house that is desolate; all spirits in it are dejected; the lamp of joy has gone out in loneliness and lamentation. Years hence you go again; there may be sobriety still, not much merriment or affluence, narrow fortunes, but a great freedom; much hard work, but the workers knowing now that they are sons and daughters of God, and content. You sit down by one of them and you hear this unhesitating confession, rising into praise to God:—"It was good for me that I lost what I loved, for it was a foolish, a selfish, an unhallowed love, hiding heaven from me. God has given me back all that was good in it, and His *own* love with it. He knew me and what I wanted better than I knew myself. I was unsteady, fickle, living only in surfaces, my passions uncontrolled, my life perverted. God took me in His mighty but merciful Hands, and shook my heart, and set me down. He shut me up in a cavern where was a darkness that could be felt. I did not see, at the time I *could* not see; I could only lie there and shiver and groan and mourn. But I see it all now. It was that I might find, and know, and trust, and love, my Father. It was that I might hear His voice out of the cloud. It was that being 'stablished, strengthened, settled,' I might learn to live, and begin to live, the life of my Lord, and live it *for* Him and with Him forever."

"O Lord, the wilderness to me
A very paradise shall be,
Since Thou for forty days wast there,
In fasting, solitude and prayer!

"Lord, let me find some lowly place
Where I may seek Thy pitying face,

And plead with Thee by Olivet,
By agony and bloody sweat.

"Some quiet aisle or dim recess
Shall make for me a wilderness;
And surely angels shall be there
To wait on penitence and prayer.

"Oh, blessed thought, that faith can see
In every altar,—Calvary,
Find there the loving arms outspread,
And fall before the fallen Head."

O GOD, blessed Son of the Everlasting Father, who lovedst them who hated Thee and sparedst them who nailed Thee to Thy cross, grant that our many and grievous offences, our unbelief and pride, our uncleanness and disobedience, and every wicked and hateful thing in us, may be atoned for by the agonies of Thy Passion, that Thou who in Thy humility didst suffer death mayest in Thy glory bestow upon us eternal light, where Thou ever livest in Thy glory with the Father and the Holy Ghost, world without end. *Amen.*

Wednesday in Holy Week.

BURIED WHEAT.

APPROACHING the cross we hear the forenotes of the cry of the Passion. Even in the commemorations of our Lord's early years there is a look and an accent of pain. It cannot be by accident; nothing that is divine is accidental. A stall-manger with oxen, the sharp end of a knife at the temple, the frightened face of a mother looking for her lost child, the bleeding doves at the purification, are signals of sacrifice. These tokens multiply as we accompany the Saviour step by step to Calvary. The pain is never arbitrary or superfluous. The suffering is borne because it lies on the way to some obedience and some triumph of good over evil, such suffering as no one would think of welcoming, except as the seed-grain of a higher kind of life and because all life is costly. It reminds us of Lacordaire's startling saying, that "the Church is born crucified,"—a paradox, no doubt, but such a paradox as prophets and mystics are apt to use when a great spiritual thought has to break through the rules of language, like St. John's expression, "the Lamb slain from the foundation of the world," or our Lord's, "He that loseth his life, for my sake, shall find it."

Keeping in mind this sacrificial aspect of our religion, because the hard places in our lives are meant to be the noblest places we find that there are, in Christ's personal ministry, what we may call critical and decisive moments, as there are with most persons who mean to be true children of God. An instance occurs just before the end. Some Greeks, representatives of a foreign nationality and a Gentile culture, come to worship at a Jewish Feast. Most likely they are irreverent travellers, inquisitive like their active-minded countrymen at home, ready to hear or see any new thing, and so not very unlike our lively populations in the west. They are of a nation easy in accommodation, and not likely to let a national prejudice stand in the way of an entertainment. The brain predominates. Turning to Philip, who by his Athenian name and temperament would attract them, they say, "Sir, we would see Jesus; introduce us to this interesting Hebrew Prophet; let us judge whether He is another of the sanguine forerunners of their Messiah, or another pretender counterfeiting Him." So then, at that moment, Greek curiosity, subtilty and skepticism, the intellectual penetration of the most intellectual of the old nations, are inquiring for the spiritual life and grace of God in the Person of the Son of Man. Who can wonder that when "Philip telleth Andrew, and Andrew and Philip tell Jesus," He exclaims in prophetic joy, "The hour is come that the Son of Man should be glorified"?

How is this new encounter met? Just as Christ always meets the question as to the way into His kingdom when put by the world, whether at its best or at its worst, by a rich young ruler or a ragged penitent in the streets, by an Athenian of that old time or an American of our time. He meets it not by lowering in the least the high condition of admittance; not by understating the cost, or hiding the hardships. This transition from exultation to warning in His language is wonderful in swiftness, in completeness. "Now is the Son of Man glorified"; but "Except a corn of wheat fall into the ground and die, it "abideth alone." "Now is my soul troubled. Shall I say, Father, save me from this hour? For this cause came I unto this hour." Taking this world as it is, men do not march out of its kingdom into the kingdom of God with trumpets and banners, or with mouths full of meat and wine. Count the cost. "Strait is the gate." Some valued thing must be given up; some easy habit must be broken with a pang; some wrench of the breaking chain must hurt us; some travail-agony be felt, before the better and nobler life can be born in the heart and grow. The Greek imagination would catch at once the meaning of the parable. Already in a fable of their mythology of the goddess of the grain mourning at the mystery of her daughter prisoned as the seed corn is under the ground, that poetic people had a faint promise, in figure, of the Christian truth. Christ opens to them in plain words the inmost heart of His Gospel. We cannot live to God, He says, except as we die to ourselves. Why not? Because life, heavenly life, whether lived in Heaven or in these earthly streets and houses, must be of love, and love always sacrifices self. God is love. There is no life yet found in the universe that is self-produced, or without an antecedent life. Science with its keenest search confesses that. But Christ is now telling us something deeper. There is no passing out of a lower sphere, He says, into a higher one, save as the inferior is in a measure sacrificed to the loftier. In her analogies, as in her laws, nature is one. The mineral kingdom disintegrates itself into the plant-world above it, where the plant-life springs out of the sod, triumphs over it, then dies, and so feeds its betters. Your grain of wheat may keep its brown, hard rind a long time as it is; you can hold it fast, hoard it, lock it up, paint it if you please, set it in gold and diamonds; these souls of men and women are doing that all the time. But then your corn of wheat "abideth alone." The man out on the farm, with a better faith, buries it, loses it, and saves it. Early and latter rain minister to it, spring mornings open it for him, setting the green blade free; summer noons ripen it; in October he comes bringing his sheaves with him.

Not only must what is bad in itself, corrupt, unjust, poisonous, perish in you, but whatever in you shuts in and stifles the better powers of love and faith, latent and asleep in you, must die too. Your uselessness "abideth alone," fulfilling no fertile mission. The glory of the seed is "fruit," and by that, Christ says, His Father is glorified. "The glory of the terrestrial is one,"—and it is not very glorious; "the glory of the celestial is another." Out of loss comes gain;

out of decay increase; out of privation abundance; out of persecutions a purer and stronger piety; out of lonely prayers of believers in worldly households, comes the "multitude that no man can number," from the grave of buried seed, resurrection; through the "strait gate" of sacrifice a great salvation. It is what the Prophet, far back, saw coming, the "valley of Achor," which means "trouble," turned into a "Door of Hope." Is it strange that the Spirit said to the faithful in Smyrna, "Fear none of those things which thou shalt suffer," and to the lukewarm in Laodicaea, "As many as I love, I rebuke and chasten"? Why otherwise should we be sobering ourselves for forty days in this subdued worship, turning our faces towards the cross?

Suffering first, satisfaction afterwards. The fruit of power and peace, gathered out of trial, comes not all at once but gradually. Ripening under a clouded sky, it ripens slowly. You are not to be discouraged by that. Almost all God's spiritual harvests come to maturity in the same silent way. That secret and gracious work of the Spirit, whatever it is, which brings tranquillity out of inward tumult, clear-sightedness out of sorrow, and sympathy for others out of your own heart-ache, goes on not by swift transformations of the inner man, or sudden reactions, but little by little. The Almighty Hand lifts your soul out of its misery as the same Hand lifts the growing blade of corn out of a black coffin in the earth to its vigorous perfection, with its blossom and grain, so imperceptibly that you see not the growth but only the fulness of life. You may lay your ear to the corn-field all the summer night and noon, where the sunshine and the rain are strengthening the stalks and weaving the leaves, but you hear no noise of the loom, or stroke of the sunbeams, or stirring of the life. Jesus said, on the eve of His passion, "Except a corn of wheat fall into the ground and die, it abideth alone; but if it die, it bringeth forth much fruit," new and multiplied and glorious life, springing from a grave. You are not blamed for your tears at the grave. Jesus wept for Lazarus. Among the ruins of your life-long plan you are not expected, the first day or the first week, to sing the *jubilate*, or forbidden to mourn. The Lord said, "My soul is exceeding sorrowful." And what He asks there is the natural cry of a human craving for companionship, "Tarry ye here and watch with me." And so the promise is a promise made to trust, not to be fulfilled at once, but "in due season." "The God of all grace, who hath called us into His eternal glory by Christ Jesus, after that ye have suffered awhile,"—after that—"Make you perfect, stablish, strengthen, settle you!" The suffering is transient, passing away. Character is permanent, abiding and settled forever. So Christ died once, but liveth evermore. Good Friday will cease with time and the world. Easter is eternal.

There is a significant symbol in one of the supernatural manifestations of our Lord's divinity as He approached His cross. We had the superb description of it by the evangelist lately, given to be read by the Church just when she turns our eyes towards this week of suffering. On Mt. Tabor, in the splendor of the Transfiguration, where Christ began to speak of the decease which He should accomplish at Jerusalem, as "the cloud" encompassed them, St. Luke says of His three timid followers, "They feared *as they entered* into the cloud." The cloud is the sign of mystery; it is the hiding of the light, it screens the sun; it veils to their sight the face of their dear Master, whose gracious countenance is to each of them as another "Sun shining in His strength." What strange obscuring, overcasting is this? Will it separate them altogether from their safe Protection? This is our own doubting question. The alarm is when the cloud comes down. It is so with the coming on of a physical disorder. Is this startling symptom the beginning of the end? The struggle is then. The sufferer thinks of the possible agonies, the lingering days of decline and nights of waking. The cloud, as he enters it, is black vapor. Imagination sees not yet the heavenly helpers, the compensations of prayer and patience and human kindness and the felt nearness of God which come after. As the malady wears on these appear with ministries almost angelic. It is so with the early sorrow of repentance, with the first crash of long-cherished schemes of fortune, with the certainty first realized that those dearer to us than ourselves must die. When mothers listen to the breathing of their fevered children, when some definite sensation pronounces all remedies vain, or medical science delivers its sentence of doom, the keepers of the house tremble, and the windows are darkened. When a guilty conscience is first roused by a conviction that the years past have been all wrong, hollow, ungrateful and ungodly, then it is an entering into the cloud, and it is a fear. Fear is a proof of weakness. In the best of Christians there is enough of it to make the moving of an approaching calamity dreadful. You shudder and start back. You ask bitterly if the cup cannot be removed, and cry that you can never, never bear it, and then you go into a secret strife with yourself, and it is the valley of the shadow of death, and you wrestle there all night, like Bunyan's Pilgrim, till the day breaketh. David said, " My sins have taken such hold upon me that I am not able to *look up*." You see no way out ; it is darkness, and nothing but darkness, around you, before you, and even above, for providence itself seems dead. Are there some who do not know this, or believe it ? We can hardly pray that they may never know it, because we are so made that only by knowing the heavy blow of pain can we know what that love is which " doth not willingly " inflict it.

For there comes, here when you suffer and are afraid, as there came on Mt. Tabor, " a voice out of the cloud," not out of a clear sky, not out of a soft and perfumed air, not out of prosperity, or gaiety, or the fulness of this world's delight, or in answer to any intellectual call. If we did not quite lose our little faith, if we kept feeling after God in the dark, and listening, we should hear Him. There was a transfiguration of the very cloud itself into a luminous tent of rest and peace. The voice says, "This is my Beloved Son; hear Him." Christ has *not* departed. Hear Him speak to you of His own Passion and decease. He will tell you that without suffering no soul is made perfect. He will say to you, "Fear none of those things which thou shalt suffer," they are friendly things. Hear Him to believe Him, and you will be willing to let the pain stay, because it is an instrument of your salvation. Hear Him to obey Him, and obedience will make you strong. Hear Him to love Him, and then, living or dying, waiting in weakness all the days of your appointed time, you will never be afraid any more, because love when it is perfect casteth fear out.

"As one who entereth by night a room
Where sufferers lie,
Shadeth his lamp to suit the languid eye,
So doth the Christ draw nigh
Unto a world of gloom.
The light of life He beareth, and doth stand
Shading it tenderly with pierced hand.
As a ploughed field,
Left desolate and bare
To winter storms and chilly, frosty air,—
Yet only thus made dreary for awhile,
That richer there, the harvest grain may smile,

So is the heart whose sod,
Tender and green,
Hath deeply been
Upturned by God.
Its sprouting blades lie low,—
Yet only broken thus by grief's ploughshare,
That in its furrows He might sow
The seed of righteousness, which shall increase
Until it yield the harvest of eternal peace."

O CHRIST, the only Lord of our salvation, who wast crucified and buried that all who follow Thee, being buried with Thee in baptism, and walking in Thy footsteps, might rise through Thee into everlasting life, keep us, we beseech Thee, that at the last we may appear before Thee clad in Thy righteousness, awaking after Thy likeness, to dwell with Thee in Thy presence and to worship Thee, the Lamb slain from the foundation of the world, with the multitude of Thy saints, world without end. *Amen.*

Thursday in Holy Week.

THE SECRET OF POWER.

THERE is no part of the New Testament which does not teach that all the members suffer or rejoice, hinder or help, together. In the great Republic of God the flocks and the pastors are meant to "have the same care one for another." We ask ourselves, and we ask one another, what can break up the religious indifference which in all this country, in all classes of men, in cities and rural districts alike, settles down on the minds of the people? For the most part, it makes no quarrel with Revelation, admits the facts of history to which the Church witnesses, and declares no hostility to Christian worship or charities, as a privilege of neighbors whose tastes happen to relish them. It does not rise to the dignity of a thinking doubt, and it does not always sink to the degradation of a vulgar sensuality. Yet it bears upon it no mark of hearty devotion, judged by any standard that our Lord has named. It does not dispute the Gospel; it lets it drop. It has objects to accomplish in a world which likes anything better than an uncompromising faith. Before this fearful mass of practical irreligion every sincere and earnest believer must stand appalled. Day and night, in dismay, disciples of the Master who are in earnest, ministers who are not hirelings, bishops who are not blind, ponder this problem. Where is the kindling and converting power? Christ says, "If any man will serve Me, let Him follow Me." But follow Him where and how? What shall His watchmen cry? Whence shall our help come?

There is a power yet to be thoroughly tried. It was tried by the holy men who, at the beginning, planted because they buried their "corn of wheat." It was tried in the ten persecutions, and wherever God gave the increase. It has been tried by innumerable saints whose "light of the world" shines along the Church's story, their names no more to be numbered than the stars in the sky. It has been tried, in our own day, by some young and older men and consecrated women in hard places near and far off, and not only in pestilences, or battle-fields, or hospitals, but in ordinary houses where martyrdom may be just as terrible, who by their faith and works and sacrifices have "obtained promises." It was proved, first of all, by Him who came traveling in the greatness of everlasting strength, who "went not up to joy, but first He suffered pain; who entered not into glory before He was crucified," whose blood healed the sick and sinful heart of our kind. It is the power of a more uncompromising, more consistent, more ardent, because more self-forgetful righteousness. If we search it to the bottom, will it not turn out to be just that "more excellent way" which St. Paul, with his radiant lamp, showed to the Corinthians in that magnificent contrast of all other "gifts" with charity? It is the power of joyful self-renunciation in the disciples, the workmen, the witnesses, of Christ. I asked a young missionary who had given up refinements, literary culture, preferments, common comforts, to live alone with sin and shame, how it could be done. "Only," he said, "only by the certainty that one is working at the side of Him who lived with lepers, publicans and paupers." It is the power of a loving as well as a living faith which rejoices and is glad to believe that, if the corn of wheat die, it bringeth forth much fruit, and that, if a man follow the Master, "where the Master is there shall the ser vant be."

One of the last things we learn is that God will abide by His own law, whether our little understanding can trace its operation or not. And here His law is that there is no possible way but the giving up of our handful of transient treasure, to reap the better fruit of Christian liberty and Christian victory afterwards. We get so used to compromises, to seeing an earthly policy mixed with the original heavenly substance; it is so common for the Church itself to be managed by worldly maxims, half bound and bandaged by secular dictation, that it strikes people as fanatical to go back and stand squarely on apostolic foundations. In spite of all this, St. Paul strengthened his young friend Timothy by telling him that "if we suffer with Christ we shall reign with Him," and though we believe it not, but deny it, "He abideth faithful and cannot deny Himself." He has been pleased to set fulfilments of that promise in the breast of mankind everywhere. For men everywhere, whatever they permit themselves to be, do admire the great givers, the givers-up, and most of all the givers who give themselves. Sometimes the people follow them alive, oftener commemorating them after they die. You can make your choice, and you do. You can keep your corn of wheat, or change it into money and keep that. People of a certain sort will then say, "Shrewd calculator! Thrifty economist! Here is a master of the art of self-preservation, here is a steward who knows how to take care of himself and his own!" But when harvest-time comes, is it harvest with him, or is it famine? The charity of self-surrender silences more infidelity, sets more reckless sinners to thinking, gathers a more willing company of listeners to the good news, than many volumes of apologetics. No sound of grander influence over every order of men in France, from prince and scholar to the rabble in the streets, issued from that spouting sea of fire and blood that bubbled at the mouths of the artillery along the barricades of Paris than the archbishop's tranquil repetition there, in the face of the mob, of the benediction of *his* King, "The Good Shepherd giveth His life for the sheep." *(Bonus Pastor animam suam dat pro omnibus suis.)* It was when the Saviour's piteous face bent down at sunset over the loathsome diseases of Capernaum that "all the city was gathered at the door."

Here then is what is given us to-day thankfully to accept into our faith. The Son of God and Son of Man is still widening out and building up for us His new kingdom on the earth,—which wherever it really comes regenerates society, and makes human life a new thing. Into that kingdom He sets the gate open. But remember this, though we may be in it there is this stern and solemn fact revealed there, to you and me, that we are not of it, and it is not in us, unless we are growing every day into its inmost principle and law; unless we are getting liberated and purified by its charity from the selfishness and pride of that other kingdom which is closer to our senses, has a louder voice, and wears a handsomer outside; unless we are contiuually looking about us to see how we can be more just to those at our side, more helpful to those that *seem* to stand below us, reverencing more and more both God and man because we see both to be one in the glorified humanity of our Lord.

We can rise, if we will, borne up by this inspiration in which the Saviour of men spoke and lived, to the very highest privilege. It was in no melancholy wailing tones that He proclaimed this necessity to His followers. "The hour is come that the Son of Man should be glorified." "I, if I be lifted up," by My cross, "will draw all men unto Me." There are states of Christian satisfaction when that which we commonly call pain is pain no more. You would not but suffer for the dear heart you love, would you? If willingness to bear a cross for another is an exact measure of affection between man and man, between man and woman, if it is true that human love is never made quite sure till vicarious anguish has gone into it, it must be just as true that there is a love like that between a saved soul and its Saviour. There may be this painless sacrifice, for aught we know, among the felicities of heaven; the smart of it lost in the closer nearness to Christ. That is the fulness of the promise: "Where I am there shall also My servant be."

We come again and again to the sacrificial feast, instituted as on this day, the seed-grain dying, the undying Fruit and Bread of Life given and received. We pray that by some stirring up of the renewing spirit in us, by a "Power" above ourselves, in this sinning nation, amidst all this self-indulgent living and faithless thinking, in these social circles which never sit in sackcloth and ashes, come feast or fast, in this half-awakened Church, too little on its knees and hence too slow on its feet—we *seem* to pray that there may be a better doing of God's blessed will. Pray it again, before you sleep to-night. Pray it not forty days, but forty times forty. What labor cannot do, prayer will; and these two are not the same thing, in spite of the old saying of St. Edmund that to labor is to pray. "Whither art thou going?" asked the Roman Emperor Valens of a trusted Christian nobleman who had worked long and hard, but in vain, to save him the State. "Out to the desert, sire," he answered, "to pray for your empire."

We need not be afraid of all the adverse forces of society or nature. Sailing towards the Holy Land, at the head of his fleet, in the midst of a terrible tempest off Sicily, Philip Augustus said to his affrighted sailors, "It is now midnight. You hear the raging of the winds over the waters. This is a slender ship. But at home the holy community at Clairvaux are just rising to enter the chapel, there before the altar of God to pray for our safety to the Lord of storms, who holds the waves in the hollow of His hand. Their intercessions will deliver us."

As an old saint said, "Bear the cross, and it shall bear thee." At the foot of Calvary the feast is spread. "Fear none of those things that thou shalt suffer." "If so be that we suffer with Him that we may be also glorified together."

"I saw red berries and the twinkling gloss
Of pointed holly leaves which, ordered, lay
On a deep lancet-window's sloping splay;
Where the stern symbol of the ensanguined Cross
Reclined on a green bed of cushioned moss.
I pondered on the sight. 'Twas Christmas Day,
And the Church smiled in festival array
To welcome Him who counted all things loss
That He might win our souls. Alas! I said—
'Tis thus we pluck the thorns from the sharp crown
Which pressed upon the Saviour's drooping head:
We take our cross, and softly lay it down:
We love the Sign, and honor it; and there
We leave the burden which we ought to bear!"

"But if, impatient, thou let slip thy cross,
Thou wilt not find it in this world again,
Nor in another; here and here alone
Is given thee to *suffer* for God's sake.
In other worlds we shall more perfectly
Serve Him and love Him, praise Him, work for Him,
Grow near and nearer Him with all delight;
But then we shall not any more be called
To suffer, which is our appointment here."

O CHRIST JESUS, pour Thy grace upon us; grant us love, purity, lowliness and patience in all trouble and distress; feed us with thy heavenly Bread; make us strong by Thy suffering; make us to love Thee with all our hearts, and so truly and without all deceit or guile to glory in Thee, our only Saviour, that we may draw all our power and blessedness from Thee alone, to whom be rendered all praise and thanksgiving in Thy Church, and world without end. *Amen.*

Good Friday.

HE THAT WAS SLAIN.

BEHOLDING Christ on the cross, some lookers-on, who seem not before to have recognized His divinity, exclaimed, "Truly this *was* the Son of God." Apart from all the manifold effects of that sacrifice, in impression, in awakening, converting and sanctifying the souls of men, and in making the world's salvation not only possible but actual, effects which rightly form the constant subject of holy instruction on this day of atonement, there is in it a distinct demonstration that the Master of mankind cannot be less than God.

Writers and thinkers of unquestionable orthodoxy and true Catholicity hold that the incarnation of God in Christ must, from the character of God, have taken place, even had there been no fall of man to be remedied, no world-wide transgression to be covered and healed. But whatever other unspeakable ends the "Word made flesh" achieved, we have an intense concern in the power of His death. "All we like sheep have gone astray," and we know of only one way back. "The law is holy, just and good," being the will of the holy, just and perfect Searcher of every heart. That is certain. Not one of us, or of mankind, is holy, just and good. We know that without being told. So the world knew no other way but the *via crucis,* the way of the cross. When John Baptist pointed to Jesus by the Jordan it was with the declaration, "Behold the Lamb of God which taketh away the sin (not only the sins) of the world." From the first the Sufferer predicted it of Himself, and of Himself as the Mediator. Mediation requires that the Mediator should contain in Himself both the estranged powers to be reconciled. He says that this death is a "ransom." The august words of eucharistic consecration fix it ineradicably in the habitual faith and reverence of believers that the atonement is wrought by Him whom the Church worships. Nor can we forget the images and their mystical yet unmistakable significance—the brazen serpent lifted up, the bread broken, the Good Shepherd giving His life for the sheep, the dying grain of wheat, the Father saying with pathethic yearning, in the parable, "They will reverence my Son."

Where is He more to be reverenced than where we behold Him to-day?

So extraordinary was the consciousness of sin immediately developed after the crucifixion under the apostolic teachers as to leave no doubt that the death itself, by its over-mastering impression of undeserved agony, awoke the very sense of guilt of which it was the only cure. This, we know, has been the effect of a direct and simple preaching of the cross all along. In all parts of the world multitudes have thus felt the first distress of remorse, the unutterable burden of estrangement, and sent up a cry of pity, not for any picture of their bad conduct, or a description of the process of repentance, but by being shown Christ on the cross. That drew from them the irrepressible confession, "Truly, this was the Son of God." In the first sermon preached in the Christian Church observe the pointed accusation, "Him ye have taken, and by wicked hands have crucified and slain." "That same Jesus God hath made both Lord and Christ." Then it was that the smitten penitents anxiously asked, "Men and Brethren, what shall we do?" This is singularly characteristic of the apostle of penitence. "Who His own self," he writes in his first epistle, "bare our sins in His own body on the tree." "Through the precious blood as of a Lamb without blemish and without spot." His references to the "body" and the "tree" indicate the close, actual and logical connection of redemption with incarnation. By St. Paul the doctrine of propitiation, another element in redemption, is pronounced with even greater frequency and urgency; and it is here that the necessity of a divine nature in the Sufferer is most apparent, no possible offering for the iniquity of the world having this propitiatory power short of the immaculate sacrifice, the sinless Son, "Delivered for our offences;" "Died for the ungodly;" "Died for our sins according to the Scriptures;" "Made sin for us who knew no sin;" "Bought with a price, even the blood." This language makes it evident that, as the ancient sacerdotal apparatus has now to be taken up into a new relation, the typical being exchanged for an actual realized character in the Eternal High Priest, so in Him all the functions of the priestly office have place. From the first His sacrificial pain, as a necessity of salvation, is foreshadowed to His followers as they are able to bear it. It is the subject of His high converse with three of them on the Mount of Transfiguration. There was an awful disclosure of it in His speechless bearing when He turned His face towards Calvary. "They were in the way going up to Jerusalem; and Jesus went before them and they were amazed; and as they followed they were afraid." Then His announcements grew explicit, specifying prophetically the particulars of His trial, scourging, sentence, execution, with His rebuke to the ambitious sons of Zebedee. "The Son of Man came to give His life a ransom for many." The atonement was the holy fire and ecstasy of the apostle's preaching. It flamed in ascriptions, salutations, lauds, doxologies, and runs through argument, instruction, exhortation. All that long, marvellous Mosaic economy prepared the moulds of thoughts which we have taken up, opened and spiritualized, and the last voices we hear, as the visions of the last of these apostles in the Apocalypse pass away before us, cry, "Worthy is the Lamb that was slain, who hath washed us in His blood!"

Deniers and doubters, impatient at these irresistible affirmations, have contemptuously cast upon them the reproach of "a blood-theology." To which it is sufficient to reply that "the blood" was on the face and side of the Son of God and in the words of His revelation before it was in any theology, and that even if you take it out of the speech and writing of theologians you will have it left just where it was, in the speech and writing of men without whom we should have no Christian theology at all.

For us here, compassed with infirmities, and in the depth of our Good Friday humiliation, it is privilege enough to render thanks and praise to Him who, "After He had one sacrifice for sins forever, sat down on the right Hand of God."

"Follow to Calvary—
Tread where He trod—
He who for ever was
Son of God.

"You who would love Him stand,
Gaze at His face;
Tarry awhile on your
Earthly race.

"As the swift moments fly
Through the Blest Week
Read the great story the
Cross will teach.

"Is there no beauty to
You who pass by
In that lone Figure which
Marks that sky?"

O JESUS, Lamb of God, crucified for our sake, who gavest Thy cheek to the smiters and Thy temples to the thorns, and wast covered with reproaches, and didst suffer the torments of the cross, grant unto us Thy unworthy servants, that by the power of Thy passion we may be able to bear the light yoke laid upon us, and learning from Thee how meek Thou art and how great Thy love is may so share in Thy sufferings that at Thy hand we may obtain the crown of Thy faithful followers, where Thou reignest in Thy glory, everlastingly. *Amen.*

Easter Even.

PATIENT EXPECTATION.

WHILE the Master rests, "all the travail of His soul and the agonies of His body being past," the Church waits. No imagination of ours can quite represent the sorrowful anxiety, the half-despairing wonder, the timid, hopeful, questioning suspense of the little company of believers during the dark interval between His last cry on the cross and the salutations of the resurrection morning. If we have followed Him reverently step by step thus far, we can almost feel the stillness of that first Easter even. One question occupies and fills these bereft hearts: Will He rise on the third day? All is staked on the answer. Is the past a reality or an illusion? Will the future be a boundless joy or an unutterable disappointment and shame? They wait.

What better thought can accompany the tender note and subdued spirit of our service than that of the duty and the blessedness of a patient expectation?

Our want of it is generally a want of faith. We wait for a person whom we believe in and are willing to trust. It is not necessary that we should comprehend Him; that would put our understanding in place of the faith; faith is not mere intellectual satisfaction. We are not to ask explanations of His delay in coming to us or answering us. That would imply that we doubt His wisdom in delaying or else His willingness to help us. "He that believeth shall not make haste." It would be presumptuous in us to compare one of God's attributes with another; but the longer I live and the more I see of what this human race of ours was made to be, and then what it is, its wrong-doing and wrong-thinking, its ingratitude and disobedience, its tyrannies and slaveries, its gluttony and waste, the foulness of its lust, the cruelty and filth and profanity of its tongues, its stinted charities and heartless prayers, its unceasing crucifixions of its Blessed Lord, and then consider how with one breath of His Omnipotence the Almighty could clean the earth of its corruption or crush the globe itself in His hand or burn it by its sleeping fires to-night,—then nothing in His majesty or His mercy is so marvellous as this: His waiting, His patience with us, with our insolent and ungrateful selfishness, with His Church, with His ministers, with myself. Must we not all marvel at it?

What is great and good, noble and beautiful, in God is noble and beautiful in His child. "They that wait upon the Lord shall renew their strength." "Wait, I say, on the Lord." The day of the Lord shall come!

But it has not come; and so impatience takes its faithless opportunity. Will the Lord arise?

Here we are, perplexed by many problems, uncertain about many questions, perhaps depressed and discouraged by many hindrances. We can renew our assurance and regain our composure only by a patient and an active expectation. Very largely our inner life is a painful struggle between a longing for what we think ought to be and an humble acceptance of what is; between the ideal and the attainment. So, even while we keep on doing our best, we have to come meekly and patiently to the confession that "we have no power of ourselves to help ourselves," that "our sufficiency is of God."

To some of us the stumbling-block to a whole-hearted, thorough-going devotion is the prevalence of disbelief; not our own disbelief so much as that of some other people who disturb us and partly because we only half know what their doubts or denials are. There is the panic of a half-told secret and the glamour of a brilliant audacity. But the disbelievers are not so many as the indifferent, and fewer still are they who venture to frame their disbelief into propositions or put its patches together into a consistent defence.

At any rate, most of us can do very little by argument, little by sounding an alarm, and less by denunciation. There is not one of us, the least, the busiest, who cannot resist and silence the atheist by a life and conversation so near the Master as to make him a defender of the Faith. Said a skeptic to Pascal, "Well, if I believed your creed, I suppose I would live a better life." Pascal answered, "Begin by living that better life, and you will come to believe my creed." That is active waiting.

Very much so it is with the terrible tide of worldliness foaming through the streets. Most of its mischief is done inside the Church. Even there it cannot kill the higher and holier life which it corrupts and insults. But its loose living and immoralities so discredit the prayers, its frivolities and feastings so mix with the names of holy things, that a Brahmin would be puzzled to tell whether the world has bought out the Church, or the Church is entertaining the world. Christ clears up the confusion. "The prince of this world cometh, and hath nothing in Me." Give him a Church full of followers with that consistent and unyielding substance, and then God and mammon will each have his own. The line will be cut where it will be seen. Instead of a promiscuous masquerade the enemies would stand embattled, front to front. "The Day of the Lord, the day of the Lord, in the valley of Decision," they on the Lord's side waiting patiently for Him,—an active expectation.

Not so many, but not a few, scandalized by the ecclesiastical and theological divisions of Christendom, and contrasting sectarian strife with the Saviour's sacrificial prayer for unity so many centuries ago, shut their eyes, hang their heads, and wonder whether, after all, there *is* a single fold, or whether there are many folds, or whether the one has many doors, watchwords and colors. Ask yourself whether this same Christ Jesus would be other than He is, and is to us, in any one of the perfect powers and glories of His divine humanity, Master, Redeemer, Friend, Intercessor, even if there were ten schisms were now there is one? I remember that a thousand years with Him are as one day. I can fix my eyes on no pledge that He has not kept. Above all, I ask, if He, who is hurt as only Infinite Pity *can* be hurt by these contentions, bears all this strife patiently, who am I that I should not wait with Him?

Some of us are more dismayed by the inequalities of rights and privileges, of welfare and security, in civil society than by the controversies of theology. In a free republic and a free church the strong and the weak ought not to be so far apart, the wage-worker from the wage-payer, the rags and hunger of the friendless half-paid woman who starves with her child, or else sells her womanhood, from the lady she is sacrificed to who fares comfortably every day. What then? He whom Mary's *Magnificat* predicted as to be, some time or other, the Equalizer of classes and callings, bringing down the mighty from their seats and exalting them of low degree; He who told the Baptist, and His neighbors in the synagogue at Nazareth, that His Gospel was first for the poor; He who lived without one luxury or useless expenditure from the manger to the cross,—still leads the race, lifts up the lowest, outwits the shrewdness of the market and the political economist, and *waits*. Who waits with Him is on His side. You say, He is out of sight. We answer, He is coming again.

Coming again? But when, and where and how? When? At such an hour as we think not. Where? It will be where they who have waited for Him and they who have pierced Him will see Him as He is. And how? No longer slowly, but as the lightning comes. Does unbelief whisper, "He delayeth"? It was when St. James had warned the unjust defrauders of the laborers of their hire, the wanton, the man of drunkenness and the woman of vanity, that he went on with words to which we can add nothing, and from which nothing can be taken away. "Be patient, therefore, brethren, unto the coming of the Lord. Behold, the husbandman waiteth for the precious fruit of the earth, and hath long patience for it, until he receive the early and latter rain. Be ye also patient; stablish your hearts; for the coming of the Lord draweth nigh."

Finally, praying,—praying, perhaps, for that advent of glorious majesty, praying for a changed lot, for a lighter load, for a lost affection, for a flickering life, for a wayward child, for a sinning or faithless soul that is called by any dear name and has gone astray—we yet see no answer. Seven times we sent up our petition from our Carmel, and the dry heat burnt sky and field as before. What then? Then bethink yourself of what Elijah did, and what came of his waiting. Listen for "the sound of abundance of rain." Prayer lives not by what we have, but by promises. Promises are "inherited" by "faith," and by that faith which is "patience." "For we are saved by hope; but hope that is seen is not hope; for what a man seeth, why doth he yet hope for? But if we hope for that we see not, then do we with patience wait for it." Be this the Easter-even watch-song in our hearts: "If we have been planted together in the likeness of His death, we shall be also in the likeness of His resurrection."

For those who may have shared these sober thoughts of Forty Days, what better blessing can we ask than that, in patient expectation they may live in the patient Master's company, serve in His service, and rest and feast with Him when they go no more out?

"'Abide with us. O Lord, our hearts' desire,
For shadows gather round earth's evening hour': —
Such voice, methinks, goes up from Minster tower,
From village steeple and from city spire,
Loud-clashing belfry, and harmonious choir.
To Heaven they speak with an appealing power,
Our myriad churches, shining with the dower

Of art's adornments and devotion's fire.
'Abide with us'—unceasingly they cry—
'As through the ages past! The world grows old;
The love of many waxes faint and cold;
But still we lift our faithful hands on high,
And feeling after Thee athwart the sky,
Upon Thy clouded Hand would fain lay hold!'"

O GOD, by whose command the order of all time runs its course, forgive, we beseech Thee, the impatience of our unbelief, make perfect that which is lacking in our faith, grant us a steady continuance in works of charity, and, while we tarry the fulfilment of Thy ancient promises, grant us to have a good hope because of Thy sure word and Thy risen and ever-living Son, Jesus Christ our Lord. *Amen.*

www.ingramcontent.com/pod-product-compliance
Lightning Source LLC
Chambersburg PA
CBHW021217270326
41929CB00010B/1164

* 9 7 8 3 3 3 7 2 6 8 9 1 6 *